Whether you are a parent, an employer, or a church leader, it's critical to acknowledge the role millennials play in the future of the church. Grant Skeldon equips us not only to understand this generation but also to connect with them in deep and meaningful relationships.

—CRAIG GROESCHEL, PASTOR, LIFE.CHURCH;
NEW YORK TIMES BESTSELLING AUTHOR

Insightful and inspiring, engaging and enlightening, here's a much needed peek into what animates the largely misunderstood millennial generation. Thanks, Grant, for helping us understand the heart of these passionate young people.

—LEE STROBEL, BESTSELLING AUTHOR, *THE CASE
FOR CHRIST* AND *THE CASE FOR MIRACLES*

Grant has become one of the leading voices on behalf of his generation. His heart to be a bridge-builder plus his keen insight on millennials make this book a necessary resource for anyone trying to engage the next generation.

—DR. TONY EVANS, PRESIDENT, THE URBAN ALTERNATIVE;
SENIOR PASTOR, OAK CLIFF BIBLE FELLOWSHIP

Grant pulls back the curtain on the hearts of America's largest and most cause-oriented generation. His insights give us the foresight to engage, learn from, and equip millennials to engage in the greatest cause of all—the glory and mission of Jesus.

—DR. DERWIN L. GRAY, LEAD PASTOR, TRANSFORMATION
CHURCH; AUTHOR, *THE HIGH DEFINITION LEADER*

I am so excited about this book bleeding into the hearts and minds of influencers everywhere! Grant has put in the work to understand and reach his peers. He is well suited to speak into the biggest challenges that we face in leading millennials. I am so thankful for his work here.

—JONATHAN POKLUDA, TEACHING PASTOR,
WATERMARK COMMUNITY CHURCH AND THE
PORCH; AUTHOR, *WELCOME TO ADULTING*

This book reads more like a missional manifesto than a work on demographics and generational preferences. Very timely! Grant is a voice that we will be hearing more from in the future.

—ALAN HIRSCH, AUTHOR; FOUNDER, 100
MOVEMENTS AND 5Q COLLECTIVE

Grant offers insight into what drives this generation, the importance of discipleship, and how we can work together to make much of Jesus. When it comes to the mission of the church, our pews are full of people wanting to "get in the fight"; this book will help make that happen.

—MATT CARTER, PASTOR OF PREACHING AND VISION,
THE AUSTIN STONE COMMUNITY CHURCH

Grant gives us a challenging but simple solution for discipling millennials. If you are interested in the future of the church, you need to read this book, and if you are interested in the "right now" of the church, you need to read this book!

—DAVE FERGUSON, LEAD PASTOR, COMMUNITY
CHRISTIAN CHURCH; AUTHOR, *HERO MAKER*

Grant has quite possibly written the most poignant book on discipleship in our time. He puts language to things I've always felt but have had trouble articulating. This book should be required reading for every Christ follower.

—BRYAN LORITTS, LEAD PASTOR, ABUNDANT LIFE
CHRISTIAN FELLOWSHIP; AUTHOR, *INSIDER/OUTSIDER*

This is so much more than a book—it is a critical brick in bridging a generation gap, finally creating the possibility for not only more understanding but also more unity, and therefore a stronger global church. This is a must-read on harnessing the power, purpose, and potential of one of the most unique generations in history.

—JORDAN DOOLEY, AUTHOR; SPEAKER;
FOUNDER, SOULSCRIPTS

Grant's prioritization of passion, purpose, and provision for individuals and wise counsel for churches within a discipleship framework is kingdom building for all who take the time to read *and* act accordingly. Thank you, Grant , for awakening in this reader a renewed focus on discipleship.

—BOB DOLL, CHIEF EQUITY STRATEGIST,
NUVEEN ASSET MANAGEMENT

Grant's wisdom and passion are far beyond his years and he is leading and guiding us all toward a healthier and fuller cross-generational understanding. This book is a resource and guidebook for so many of us, especially leaders in the church, as we seek to communicate the gospel well to each generation.

—ANNIE F. DOWNS, BESTSELLING AUTHOR,
100 DAYS TO BRAVE AND *LOOKING OR LOVELY*

Grant has written a book that is filled with vibrant truth. His heart and yearning to see a generation come to know Jesus is apparent throughout each and every page.

—JARRID WILSON, PASTOR; AUTHOR, *LOVE IS OXYGEN*

The Passion Generation will open your eyes and heart to the incredible gift of millennials—they're positioned and ready to grow the church, the gospel and the community of faith in ways you've never imagined. A timely, engaging, and thoughtful work.

—MARGARET FEINBERG, AUTHOR, *FIGHT BACK WITH JOY*

Grant is a proven leader in the Dallas community committed to engaging millennials in city transformation empowered by the gospel. This book is a must read for any leader who loves millennials and desires to see them reach their full potential.

—BRYAN CARTER, SENIOR PASTOR, CONCORD CHURCH

THE PASSION GENERATION

THE SEEMINGLY RECKLESS, DEFINITELY DISRUPTIVE, BUT FAR FROM HOPELESS MILLENNIALS

GRANT SKELDON

WITH RYAN CASEY WALLER

ZONDERVAN

The Passion Generation
Copyright © 2018 by Grant Skeldon and Ryan Casey Waller

Requests for information should be addressed to:
Zondervan, *3900 Sparks Dr. SE, Grand Rapids, Michigan 49546*

ISBN 978-0-310-35185-6 (softcover)

ISBN 978-0-310-35279-2 (audio)

ISBN 978-0-310-35189-4 (ebook)

Cover design: Jeff Miller | Faceout Studio
Cover photo: © photominus / iStock
Interior art: Emily Mills
Interior design: Denise Froehlich

First printing August 2018 / Printed in the United States of America

Contents

Topical Contents

Skip around if you'd like.

CHAPTERS HELPFUL FOR PARENTS

CHAPTERS HELPFUL FOR PASTORS

CHAPTERS HELPFUL FOR BUSINESS LEADERS

CHAPTERS HELPFUL FOR MILLENNIALS

Acknowledgments

Kevin Batista

Sujo John

Raymond Harris

Eric Swanson

Mac Pier

Gary Brandenburg

Charles Spurgeon

Martin Luther

Dr. Adam Wright

Jerry Wagner

Margie Frank

Dimas Salaberrios

Scott Sheppard

Sally Squib

George Mueller

William Wilberforce

Online Experience at PassionGen.Online

We live in a time when there are several options for taking in a good book, from print books to audio books to ebooks. But I'm taking it a step farther.

The Passion Generation is riddled with references to videos I've handpicked to amplify and reinforce your reading experience. Each video is embedded in order on the book site: **PassionGen.Online**.

Wherever you see the device icon:

1. Simply pull up PassionGen.Online on your phone or laptop.
2. Scroll to the matching video number from the book page.

The videos in this book are must-see material—some informative, some inspiring, some sobering, and some that are just downright funny—but all of them will help you get the most out of *The Passion Generation*, so don't miss out!

PART I

DISCIPLING
MILLENNIALS

CHAPTER 1

THE GENERATION GAP

March 8, 2006, was the biggest day of my life.

Before I tell you why, allow me to tell you a little about myself. I was sixteen years old, and like most high school kids, I found my identity in something other than God. To me, Jesus was a good guy and I knew he was real, but I didn't want him yet. He was nice, but he also was a killjoy. I wanted to have fun first and then settle down later. I told myself, "I'll be a Christian when I'm twenty-six." I'm not kidding. I planned an age to become a Christian. It was pretty ridiculous, but it reveals how much I didn't get it.

God didn't sit on the throne of my heart. Instead I replaced him with typical substitutes. First, it was basketball. I had always loved the sport and been identified as a basketball player. My friends and I played all the time. Second, there was my girlfriend. We had been together for three years (which is basically forever in teenage years), so everyone thought we were going to be high school sweethearts. She was the girl on the hip-hop team, and I was the guy on the basketball team. It was like a ghetto *High School Musical* in the making.

And yes, you heard that correct: my school had a hip-hop team. It's probably a good time to tell you that I grew up in a part of Dallas that was a little more urban, which is a euphemism for growing up with a lot of Hispanics and African Americans. This was pretty awesome, because I'm Hispanic and African American. My mom is a five foot little Mexican lady, and my dad is a six foot four South African man. They're definitely a unique duo. But I'll be honest. I feel like a Mexi*cant*, because I can't speak any Spanish. And my dad is white, so he's not what people expect when I tell them he's from Africa. (Once when I spoke in Uganda, I joked that I was *technically* African American, but when I told them my dad was South African, they laughed and said, "That doesn't count!") My upbringing is important for you to know, because the third thing on the throne of my heart was the approval of people. I, like many high school kids, cared a lot about what people thought of me. I just wanted to fit in and be liked, but it's hard to fit in when you always feel different. Our culture shapes a lot about us: food, dress, music, hobbies, values. Being Mexican but not feeling Mexican, and being South African but not feeling South African, made it pretty hard to figure out my identity. *Who am I? What am I supposed to be like when I'm diverse and everyone else isn't?*

Luckily, my high school was radically diverse. So for the first time in a long time, I felt like I belonged. Things were great. Our basketball team was good, my girlfriend was legit, and I had just landed my first job at my favorite clothing store, Marshalls. I was living the dream.

Then, in one week, everything came crashing down.

On Monday, my girlfriend cheated on me. On Wednesday, I was kicked off the basketball team. And by Friday, my popularity was washed down the drain. Everyone was talking about me, but not the way I wanted them to. I know it sounds dramatic, but from my limited teenage perspective, life was over. Everything I had been passionate about and everything I had placed my identity in was gone.

I had no girlfriend to spend time with. No basketball practice to attend. No friends to go see. Just gossip to avoid and feelings to numb. So when I got invited to a youth group I had never been to before, I accepted the invitation.

I wasn't really interested in finding God, but I was now single, and I was told there were hot girls there, so I went. It wasn't my first time in church, but it was the first time I went of my own volition. I had attended only when my mom dragged my brothers and me along. It wasn't that I hated church. But I definitely didn't like it. I just had never really connected with anyone there. Like most millennials, I craved authenticity, and the church just didn't seem authentic at all.

But that night, church went from being fake to being the most hopeful place on earth. For the first time, I heard the good news in a way that was real to me. I realized that the reason I was in shambles was because I had placed my identity in things that wouldn't matter in eternity. My whole life unraveled in one week because God wasn't my foundation. I was tired of trying to earn the approval of man instead of simply receiving the approval of God. So on March 8, 2006, I placed my future in the hands of a God who would never leave me.

The very next day, God gave me back my girlfriend, my spot on the team, and my popularity.

Okay, that didn't happen. God didn't give me my old life back, and in the end I didn't want it anymore. I had him, and I didn't need anything else.

The crazy thing about God is he can change your life without changing your circumstances. After my conversion, I returned to the same heartache that crushed me, but I was different inside. God was now in me. And I didn't care anymore about what people thought. Leonard Ravenhill once said, "A man who is intimate with God will never be intimidated by man." I didn't know it at the time, but God was just getting started. It wouldn't be his last intervention.

THE SECOND MOST IMPORTANT DAY OF MY LIFE

The next year was full of culture shock. I was in a whole new world and just trying to learn how to respond to it. I mean, God got me ten years earlier than I had planned! I went from a basketball team where most of my friends were black to a church community where all my friends were white. You can hang out in a group for only so long before you start trying to live like them and look like them. I started wearing American Eagle. I started wearing Hollister. I traded my baggy jeans for skinny jeans with holes in them. I went the whole nine yards. You have to understand, no one at my church dressed like the kids at my school. So I adapted. The funny thing is I didn't just change the way I dressed. I also changed the places I ate. I don't know if this is a white thing or a Christian thing, but I discovered the second trinity of the church: Starbucks, Chipotle, and Chick-fil-A. All places I had never been before I started hanging out with white Christians. (Don't lie. You know you've been to at least one of these places in the last three days.)

Fast-forward two weeks from the night I was saved, and we come to the second most important day of my life—the day discipleship began.

A man in the new church I was attending, a guy named Kevin Batista, heard I had given my life to Christ. He sought me out to challenge me to follow him as he followed Christ.

The following pattern is critical to everything else I am going to say. If you don't learn anything else from this book, just make sure you get this pattern. I promise it will make all the difference. Here it is:

- Jesus invited me to follow him.
- I accepted Jesus' invitation.
- Kevin, who had been following Jesus longer than I had, invited me to follow him as he followed Jesus.
- I accepted Kevin's invitation.

I followed him as he followed Christ. I had no idea how important it is for a young Christian to be discipled by an older and more mature believer. Heck, I didn't even know what discipleship is! Thank God Kevin did. I thank God even more that Kevin didn't just know about discipleship but had dedicated his life to *doing it*. And not the kind of cheap discipleship that has become so commonplace in today's church. Kevin was into the real-deal discipleship modeled by Jesus in the Gospels.

What do I mean by that?

Well, most Christians think of discipleship as simply a meeting over coffee to pray, read the Bible, and share a little bit about life. Of course, there's never been anything wrong with some good ol' Scripture, a triple shot of espresso, a couple of high fives, and goodbyes. Coffee and conversation are awesome things to do with one another. But coffee and conversation aren't discipleship. Jesus didn't invite the disciples to go have coffee with him. He invited them to go do life with him. So Kevin and I didn't really do the whole coffee and conversation thing. Over the year and a half that Kevin discipled me, we probably met one-on-one only two or three times.

> Coffee and conversation aren't discipleship.

Kevin wasn't interested in inviting me to a quick catch-up on the week. He wasn't interested just in who I was dating or how many quiet times I had. He wanted to know about my *entire* life, and he wanted to invite me into his. So that's what we did together: life.

Kevin pulled back the curtain on his reality, not limiting our time together to an hour before the real day began or an hour after it had already ended. He didn't give me his leftovers. He gave me the main course. Kevin didn't want me just to know something new; he wanted me to be something new. He invited me to leadership meetings, to social gatherings, to his small group, even into time with his family. He gave me the opportunity to really see into his life. He didn't just show me what he wanted me to see. He let me see all of it—the good, the bad, and the ugly. And look, some of it was good. Some of it was bad. And some of it was ugly. But all of it was real. And that's what I needed.

Even so, the more I saw, the more I realized I wanted to be like him. Was he perfect? No. But was he trying hard to be like Jesus? Definitely.

I define discipleship as this: frequently following someone who is spiritually a step ahead.

I earnestly wanted to know the Bible like Kevin did. I wanted to love strangers like Kevin did. I wanted someday to be a good husband and father like Kevin was. I wanted to love Jesus like Kevin loved Jesus. And eventually, I wanted to disciple someone like Kevin discipled me.

A lot of people complain about this generation. "They're job hopping. They're prolonging adolescence. They're slacktivists. They're still living in my home!" But I got from Kevin what few young people get, and that's perspective. Young people may be different from generations before, but if they watch most of their friends making all the same mistakes, it doesn't seem like a mistake. It just seems like a natural part of life. That's where the church should be different. Because discipleship disrupts division. It's a bridge between generations. It gives perspective, vision, and wisdom to those coming up. When Kevin let me see his life, he let me see my potential. Until him, I was just doing what was right in my own eyes.

There's a saying: "We all learn from our mistakes." But no one said we have to learn from *our own* mistakes. I've tried to save time by gaining wisdom from the mistakes of those before me, but that became possible only through the corridor of discipleship.

Most were saved when they were young, but few were discipled when they were young.

Beyond the saving grace of Christ, Kevin's willingness to pour into me is what has made all the difference. It was the left lane of sanctification for me. He led me, which has allowed me to lead others. If it weren't for him, I think I would have spiritually wandered for years, trying to figure out, "What do I do next?" And this is what happens to most young people. Most Christians give their lives to Christ before the age of eighteen. But here's what I've found. Most were saved when they were young, but few were discipled when they were young. Many were never discipled at all.

THE COMMON DENOMINATOR AMONG YOUNG INFLUENCERS

I know I'm not the only one who has experienced how formative discipleship is. From what I've seen, discipleship is the common denominator in the lives of young Christians who grow into great leaders.

Show me a twentysomething leading a nationally impactful ministry or business, and I'll show you someone who had an older, wiser person pour into them. Someone gave them responsibilities they didn't earn and opportunities they didn't deserve. Someone let them fail. Someone challenged them. Someone was willing to let them see their junk and believed in them enough to say the same courageous words Jesus said to his disciples so long ago: "Come. Follow me."

Under every great young leader is a great foundation of mentors. Shouting this truth from the rooftops is my primary motivation for writing this book, because the church is not doing well with young people. Everyone knows this. What people don't know is that the solution is so much simpler than we think.

Too often people ask me to help them reach millennials, and I can tell when they're really just

> Under every great young leader is a great foundation of mentors.

looking for tips and tricks. But my answer is old school. My answer is discipleship. If you want to reach every generation from now until Jesus comes back, disciple someone who disciples someone who disciples someone who disciples someone . . . You get the picture.

Better Together

The longer we go without taking discipleship seriously, the wider the chasm between our generations will become. And let's be honest, the chasm is already wide. What I witness in my daily work is that both generations are really turned off by each other. Older people think millennials are lazy and entitled. Millennials think older people just want to criticize them. The tension has gotten so bad that I sometimes worry we are about to give up on one another altogether. But we can't do that, because the truth is that we desperately need each other.

Should I say that again? I probably should. I know the generations are frustrated, but the proper way forward is not apart but together. A house divided cannot stand. The church has never done well when it fractures over minor issues. We are always stronger when we blend and when we highlight what we have in common: Christ. We'll talk more about this later, but for now I just want to remind us that in Christ, we can overcome any manner of difference. In the past, the church has overcome matters of much greater dispute than simple clashes between generations. So take heart, there is a lot of reason for hope.

With that throat clearing out of the way, let's get down to some business.

Look, I am a millennial, and I'll be the first to admit that if we're left to our own devices, my generation will go full-blown *Lord of the Flies* trying to raise ourselves. And we all know what happens when young people make the rules. Piggy dies. So many millennials are doing this, and it is not going well for us. In 2015, the American Psychological Association reported that the millennial generation is the most stressed-out generation in America. We desperately need the wisdom of older generations, a wisdom we have not been particularly good at seeking out.

We also need to apologize to the older generations for acting so entitled. We have so much to be grateful for, and we owe it all to the hard work of previous generations. We need to express our gratitude. We are working on it. Everywhere I go, I repeat this message to my generation. But if you've never heard a millennial apologize, please hear it from me. We are sorry. I pray you'll forgive us. We have made some big mistakes, and we are nowhere near perfect. We may like to play it cool on the outside, but there is a lot of anxiety underneath the surface.

My consistent prayer for this book is that it will be more than a book. I want it to be a bridge. Only the Enemy wins when we are divided. Yes, we are different, but we don't have to be divided. I think we can find a way to leverage our differences for good. But before we get there, we're going to need some honest dialogue. So let's talk.

The older generations, for their part, need to cut down on their criticism of millennials. I mean, for real, it's open season on us these days. I don't know if there is a group in America you're more awarded for making fun of than millennials. And this isn't me with thin skin. This is me seeing people constantly voicing their disdain for millennials and then complaining that they can't reach them. I know we can be difficult to understand. I know we love our iPhones and expensive coffee and flexible work schedules. And I know that all this can irritate you if you're older. But the one way to guarantee you will never understand us is to criticize us without spending time with us. We can't care for each other as individuals if we judge each other as generalizations. It has always been kindness, not criticism, that leads people to repentance. In all sincerity, we need you.

> You can't expect what you don't invest. It's pretty hard to grow up without grown-ups.

So I do have a hard request.

If you're not discipling anyone, will you please refrain from criticizing the next generation?

You can't expect what you don't invest. It's pretty hard to grow up without grown-ups.

I would even say you're part of the problem. You're throwing rocks from a distance, and you're not even in the game. We reap what we sow. This isn't new. You've neglected discipleship, and you're surprised by the results? It's like a farmer criticizing his crops for not growing, even though he never waters them. Something needs to change.

We need to change.

Kevin understood that I needed him before I even knew I needed him. I don't know where I would be today if he hadn't engaged me. He made me one of the lucky millennials. Sometimes I refer to millennial leaders as unicorns because people think we don't exist, especially in the church. I mean, when only three out of every ten millennials attend church, it can be slim pickings to find leaders there. But we do exist.

But we might not be here tomorrow if we can't come together today. We are about to have a generational baton pass. And I'd hate for our lead to count for nothing simply because we didn't sync up when passing the baton. An African proverb says, "If you want to go fast, go alone. If you want to go far, go together."

We've tried alone, and it doesn't seem to work. What would it hurt to try together?

Chapter 1, "When Passing the Baton Goes Wrong"

MOST WERE **SAVED** WHEN THEY WERE YOUNG, **BUT FEW WERE DISCIPLED** WHEN THEY WERE YOUNG.

DISCIPLESHIP DISRUPTS DIVISION

If you're **NOT** DISCIPLING anyone, will you please refrain from criticizing the next **GENERATION?**

YOU CAN'T **EXPECT** WHAT YOU DON'T **INVEST.**

IT'S PRETTY HARD TO GROW UP WITHOUT GROWNUPS.

WHAT MILLENNIALS WANT

Before we dive deeper into discipleship, let's briefly address the elephant in the room—the most likely reason you opened this book in the first place.

Millennials. Who are they? What do they want? You want to know more about millennials, because you parent them or work with them and because you know they are crucial to the future of the church. Listening to one another and learning about one another is the first step toward bridging the generation gap.

Okay, so a bit on millennials. First of all, we are everywhere. Born roughly between 1982 and 2004, millennials are now the nation's largest living generation. It's projected that by 2050, there will be more than 79 million millennials in the US.[1] That's a lot of skinny jeans and iPhones.

Or maybe not. There's a lot of generalizations about millennials. Since this is the largest and most diverse generation in human history, there are many groups within this group. I've found Boston Consulting Group's categories to be helpful in considering the different types of millennials. (See next page.)

It's nearly impossible to log in to Facebook these days or watch the news without hearing something about millennials, usually a question laced in frustration:

- Why don't you vote?

Hip-ennial

"I can make the world a better place."

- Cautious consumer, globally aware, charitable, and information hungry
- Greatest user of social media but does not push/contribute content

Gadget Guru

"It's a great day to be me."

13%

- Successful, wired, free spirited, confident, and at ease
- Feels this is his best decade
- Greatest device ownership, pushes/contributes to content
-

29%

Millennial Mom

22%

"I love to work out, travel, and pamper my baby."

- Wealthy, family oriented, works out, confident, and digitally savvy
- High online intensity
- Highly social and information hungry
- Can feel isolated from others by her daily routine

Clean and Green Millennial

10%

"I take care of myself and the world around me."

- Impressionable, cause driven, healthy, green, and positive
- Greatest contributor of content, usually cause related
-
-
-

Anti-Millennial

16%

"I'm too busy taking care of my business and my family to worry about much else."

- Locally minded, conservative
- Does not spend more for green products and services
- Seeks comfort and familiarity over excitement/change/interruption

Old-School Millennial

10%

"Connecting on Facebook is too impersonal; let's meet up for coffee instead!"

- Not wired, cautious consumer, and charitable
- Confident, independent, and self-directed
- Spends least amount of time online, reads

Graphic reproduced from The Boston Consulting Group, *www.bcg.com/documents/file103894.pdf*. Used with permission.

- Why are you waiting so long to get married?
- Why can't you find a job after graduation?
- Why are you so obsessed with your phone?

And the big one for the church:

- Why are you abandoning us?

For the purposes of this book, I'll focus primarily on the last one. Why are young people leaving the church?

I won't lie to you. The statistics are frightening. While roughly 70 percent of Americans continue to identify as Christian, more than a third (35 percent) of millennials now describe themselves as being unaffiliated with any particular religion.[2] This means that when asked to select their religion from a list, a full 35 percent of them selected "none of the above." This is way more than members of Generation X who were unaffiliated at a comparable point in their life cycle (20 percent) and twice as many as baby boomers who were unaffiliated at the same point (13 percent).

So that's not great news.

Moreover, the Barna Group performed a similar study and found that a shocking 59 percent of millennial Christians who grew up in the church are no longer attending church, and less than half of all millennials (47 percent) have attended church in the last six months.[3]

Of the millennials who no longer attend church, a massive majority hold negative views of Christians. Consider the following numbers.

- 87 percent view Christians as judgmental.
- 85 percent view Christians as hypocritical.
- 91 percent view Christians as anti-homosexual.
- 70 percent view Christians as insensitive to others.[4]

Ouch.

In the book *UnChristian*, David Kinnaman and Gabe Lyons write, "Our research shows that many of those outside Christianity, especially younger adults, have little trust in the Christian faith, and esteem for the lifestyle of Christ followers is quickly fading among outsiders. They admit their emotional and intellectual barriers go up when they are around Christians, and they reject Jesus because they feel rejected by Christians."[5]

This, in a nutshell, is what the church is up against. Millennials often are not only apathetic to the church but also openly hostile.

This becomes more worrisome when you consider how fast this opinion has developed. In 2007, the religious "nones" represented only 16 percent of the population. In the seven years following, that number ballooned to 23 percent. The nones have become the second-largest group in America's religious economy. Are you tracking with me on this? The second-largest group in America's religious economy is a group that claims to have no religion at all. This fact cannot be ignored. The nones are a serious issue. What makes them even more serious is that they shot up the list at a time when the Christian share of the US population fell from 90 percent to 71 percent.

So what does all this mean? What is happening? And is there any hope for the church?

Well, on its face, it does appear our country is becoming more secular, especially among young people. For those born between 1990 and 1996, 56 percent identify as Christians. Compare that with the 86 percent of those born between 1928 and 1945, and you can begin to feel the seismic nature of this shift. Young people are walking away from faith. There's just no getting around it. The reality, however, is not as simple as the numbers or Facebook headlines suggest.

REJECTING THE CHURCH

We can't ignore how many of the religious nones have spiritual habits—they pray, they believe in God, and they believe in the afterlife. Only a third of them explicitly identify as atheists. The rest of them are spiritual, but they're just not sure if they like religion. That's where the majority of nones find themselves. They want God, but they don't want the way the church has given them God.

In 2013, millennial author Rachel Held Evans published an article on CNN called "Why Millennials Are Leaving the Church." She wrote this:

> What millennials really want from the church is not a change in style but a change in substance.
>
> We want an end to the culture wars. We want a truce between science and faith. We want to be known for what we stand for, not what we are against.
>
> We want to ask questions that don't have predetermined answers.
>
> We want churches that emphasize an allegiance to the kingdom of God over an allegiance to a single political party or a single nation.
>
> We want our LGBT friends to feel truly welcome in our faith communities.
>
> We want to be challenged to live lives of holiness, not only when it comes to sex, but also when it comes to living simply, caring for the poor and oppressed, pursuing reconciliation, engaging in creation care and becoming peacemakers.[6]

It is an oversimplification to say millennials have rejected the church and are moving on. The reality is that they have some beef with the church—a beef that could always be resolved (something I try to do in part 2, "What Millennials Look For in Church"). The fact that millennials are upset with the church is hopeful news, because it means that when we hear the category "none," we can't assume the person is an atheist. For all we know, he or she appreciates the concept of church but has been profoundly disappointed by it. But look, when nearly 70 percent of millennials say they are spiritual and 21 percent fess up to praying every day, there are a lot of reasons to remain positive.

So the rash conclusion is that an entire generation has decided to reject the church. But as you can see, it's not that simple. Millennials aren't really rejecting the church so much as rejecting what the church has called them to. Or better yet, what the church has failed to call them to.

The church has called millennials to join the church. Millennials, however, want to *be* the church.

What do I mean?

The church wants millennials to show up on Sunday, volunteer when we can, and tithe—just like our parents and grandparents did. But that bar is too low. It's not compelling. There's this idea that millennials will leave the church if we call them to do too much. Well, I think they're leaving the church because we call them to do too little. The world is giving bigger responsibilities than the church! Today if a young person joins the military, they are entrusted with a lethal weapon on foreign soil. Likewise, if a young person joins a nonprofit, they may be allowed to run an entire program overseas. But if a young person joins the church, they are placed on the parking team, the greeting team, or the children's ministry. The world is saying, "Let's go, right now." The church is saying, "Slow down, just wait." I think the church is the right place with the wrong urgency, and the world is the wrong place with the right urgency. Jesus had urgency. He said the kingdom of heaven is at hand. He also gave huge responsibilities to young people who didn't deserve it. He gambled *everything* on the disciples.

> Millennials are leaving the church not because we ask them to do too much but because we ask them to do too little.

I'm not trying to shame anyone, but if we're going to get to the bottom of this issue, then we have to speak openly and honestly about it. I remember speaking at a conference to a bunch of Christian business leaders. One of the CEO's kids came up to me afterward and said, "I love what you did there. You gave them the truth, nicely. You basically just served them chocolate-covered vegetables!"

There's going to be a lot of chocolate-covered vegetables along this journey, because we've gotten to an unhealthy place. The next generation is in trouble. Actually, the church in America is in trouble. There's this idea that the church will never die. And that's true. But I think we need to wake up to the fact that the church in America *will die* if we don't change. If you've ever been to Israel, you'll be shocked to see how few churches are there, and that's where Jesus started everything!

God goes where his people are hungry. He never forces himself on us. If his people don't want him, he'll go somewhere else. So much church history is in Europe, but today it's just that—history. Europe once was at the center of the Reformation, but now the church there is a shell of what it used to be. Then God moved in mighty ways in the formation of our country. From the Second Great Awakening to Billy Graham crusades, there was a hunger in our nation, but all the numbers now point to a decline in the church in the United States.

Yet don't worry, the church will never die. God goes where his people are hungry, even desperate, for him. Just listen to the stories of people coming to faith in the Middle East, in Asia, and in South America. The church is alive and well. We're always one generation away from extinction, and I'm not trying to be doom and gloom here. I'm looking at history and seeing a pattern. The church will never die, but it's never promised to one specific location. Like Nineveh, we need to wake up.

> The church will never die, but it's never promised to one specific location.

My prayer is that our appetite begins to desire the healthier, harder things in life that line up with the Scriptures and contrast our culture. My prayer is for confession, repentance, and expectation. If you haven't noticed by now, this book isn't so much about how to reach millennials as about how to be the church God designed us to be. I just happen to believe that millennials are longing for that kind of church.

WORLD CHANGERS

So what is it that millennials want? Here it is in a nutshell: millennials want to change the world. They want a cause to fight for and a community to belong to.

We have come of age during a time of great social, spiritual, and economic upheaval, and we just are not content to keep the status quo. We want to leave this world in better shape than we found it, and nothing is going to stop us. Not a bad economy. Not student debt. Not even the little god of distraction Steve Jobs invented.

Our heroes are people who think outside the box and relentlessly pursue their passions in life, regardless of their circumstances. We aren't motivated by finding security in life. We are motivated by making a difference. An Intelligence Group survey found that "64 percent of millennials say they would rather make $40,000 a year at a job they love than $100,000 a year at a job they think is boring."[7]

Everyone is talking about millennials, but no one is *listening* to them. For only so long can I watch people talk about millennials as if they were whales. *They're migrating here! They're no longer there! When will they ever come up for air! They. They. They.*

I wrote this book because everyone is talking about millennials . . . except millennials. So much research! But so little results. Older generations can provide interesting and accurate analysis of the millennial generation. But what one generation cannot do for another is fully understand their experience. I'm shocked at how often I see nonmillennials speaking on behalf of millennials. It's like men speaking on behalf of women or white people training other white people on how to reach black people. Fortunately, there is a distinguishing difference between whales and millennials.

Millennials can talk. Which means we can answer the questions everyone is asking.

So let me tell you one thing that we are saying. Or rather one thing we keep asking ourselves: "How am I going to make an impact in the world, and what is my purpose?"

This question is at the core of a well-known book titled *The Purpose Driven Life*. A pastor named Rick Warren wrote it, and it's sold more than forty million copies. Everyone from the Mexican drug lord "El Chapo" to Kim Kardashian has supposedly read it. Michael Phelps told ESPN the book convinced him not only of the existence of God but also that he had a purpose in life.

Wait. Stop.

What did Phelps say? Michael Phelps didn't know he had a purpose in life? *The* Michael Phelps? The same man who trained relentlessly for decades to win more Olympic gold medals than any other person in history? That guy didn't know he had a purpose in life?

What the what?

Olympians are arguably the most purpose-driven people on earth. For years, sometimes decades, they orient their entire lives around the pursuit of a single goal. There is no ambiguity in their lives whatsoever. They train to win. Period. What they eat, how much they sleep, everything they do is centered on this one goal. Faster. Higher. Longer. Stronger. The purpose of an Olympian's life could not be clearer: win. After years of training and winning, how could Michael Phelps be uncertain about his purpose in life?

Because.

He's a millennial.

Just kidding. Millennials are obsessed with the question of life's purpose. What on earth am I here for?

This is *the* question for millennials and the starting point for understanding an often-misunderstood generation. If you happen to be a millennial, my guess is that you agree with this sentiment. If you aren't a millennial, my guess is that you've encountered this purpose obsession in your home, church, or office. The millennial obsession with purpose is not even close to a secret, though it's rarely understood and even more rarely seen as a positive attribute.

Consider Tom Brady at twenty-seven years old in his *60 Minutes* interview: "Why do I have three Super Bowl rings and still think there's something greater out there for me? I mean, maybe a lot of people would say, 'Hey, man, this is what it is.' I reached my goal, my dream, my life. Me, I think, God, it's gotta be more than this."

He's then asked, "What's the answer?" To which Brady replies, "I wish I knew. I wish I knew."

▶ CHAPTER 2, "TOM BRADY LOOKING FOR PURPOSE"

Like Michael Phelps, Tom Brady accomplished in his professional career what no one has before. And yet he was unsatisfied because he was uncertain about his purpose. For me, this illustrates that millennials are not willing to trade purpose for anything, not even fame and fortune. It also shows that mastering a craft and having a purpose are not the same. Millennials will remain restless until they have a clear answer as to why they are here.

Whether it's Tom Brady asking the question or a twenty-year-old college dropout still living in his parents' basement, my answer is always the same. The purpose of a millennial's life is the same as every other person's life in this world.

To know God and to make him known.

In other words, the Great Commandment plus the Great Commission.

"Don't say God is silent when your Bible is closed." That's what my friend Matt Brown says. God's will is not a mystery. It's not a secret. His commission to Adam and Eve in the beginning is similar to his commission to the disciples in the end: Go and multiply. Go and make disciples.

This generation is hungry for a movement. They want to change the world. Let's introduce them to the only real movement there's ever been—the gospel advancing through the church. There is no greater movement. It's the Great Commission. And what I love about discipleship is that Jesus didn't just tell us what to do. He *showed* us.

CHAPTER 3

PASSION, PURPOSE, AND PROVISION

I probably see too many movies. There, I said it. Confession made. I can't help it. Seriously, I love every aspect of the experience. The smell of popcorn, the hushed voices, the anticipatory dark, and the rush of adventure when the screen finally bursts into technicolor life. The thing is I don't just watch movies. I dissect them. I study them. I've never watched a movie I haven't learned a lesson from. I don't fly Spirit because *Titanic* taught me to choose my transportation wisely. I learned from *Forrest Gump* to just say yes and enjoy the ride. And the movie *Jaws* taught me to *never* get in the water. No. Matter. What.

One of my favorite movies, though, is *Dead Poets Society*. There's a lot to be learned from this movie when it comes to millennials. In the movie, Robin Williams plays professor John Keating, a teacher desperately committed to encouraging young men to pursue their passion and purpose in life. But he teaches at an exclusive college prep school that is primarily focused on the provision mindset: landing a good job that will pay lots of money. The goal of the school is to graduate these boys into Ivy League colleges, where they will go on to become doctors and lawyers. Anything less than this kind of future is considered a failure.

In the movie, Mr. Perry pressures his son Neil to drop his

extracurricular pursuits in order to focus more on his studies so he can make it into college and then medical school. But Neil loves working on the yearbook and acting in the school play. Neil has a big decision to make. Does he listen to his father, let a piece of himself die inside, and always wonder, "What if?" Or does he disobey his father, go behind his back, and pursue things he's passionate about?

I want to point out that Mr. Perry isn't trying to crush Neil with his rules. In his mind, he's trying to save Neil from a childish and naive decision. Mr. Perry is focused on questions of provision and can find no place for Neil's focus on passion and purpose. At one point, Mr. Perry declares, "After you've finished medical school and are on your own, then you can do as you please. But until then, you do as I tell you. Is that clear?" His single-minded drive crushes Neil's dreams, and as those who have seen the movie know, the consequences are tragic.

Dead Poets Society, besides being a great movie, illustrates one of the biggest reasons for the generation gap between millennials and their parents. And it all has to do with how both generations view the three words embodied by Neil and his father: passion, purpose, and provision.

American Dream or Millennial Nightmare?

The old (and outdated) pattern for life is that people focused on provision first, before dealing with questions of passion and purpose. This is Mr. Perry's assumption about life. Young people must receive an education in order to secure a job that allows them to achieve the American Dream: steady career, happy marriage and family, house, church membership, pension, and peaceful retirement. In a word, success. Once they were successful, they could begin to think about the passion and the purpose of their lives, or what they could do to make their lives significant. Another great example of this old way of thinking is Bob Buford's bestselling book *Halftime: Moving from Success to Significance.* Buford's premise is

MID-LIFE CRISIS:

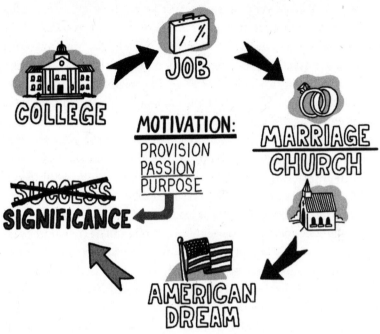

that many people spend the first half of their lives chasing financial success until they encounter a midlife crisis, then realize that something is missing and spend the second half of their lives pursuing significance, not just success.

Millennials, however, have seen their parents and grandparents go through this halftime experience, and they're wondering if they want the same.

Worse, the old system is broken. All these stages of life might have worked in the past, but times have changed. The American Dream is starting to feel like a millennial nightmare.

- *College.* Has anyone noticed that these days, colleges have a better guarantee of putting your kids in debt than getting them a job? Fifty-one percent of millennials are underemployed.

They have a job, but not a job related to their degree or with the income they expected and need.

▪ *Job.* A lot of young people never knew their dad because he chose work over his family. Worse, it didn't even seem to give him life. It took all his time, energy, and joy, and in return it just paid the bills. Also, I often get asked why millennials aren't loyal to their companies like people used to be. My question is, "Do you feel like companies are still loyal to their employees like they used to be?"

▪ *Marriage.* Has any generation in the last hundred years witnessed more divorce than this one? And they say we're noncommittal. I think they want to make the right decision.

▪ *House.* Ever hear of the housing bubble? Upside-down mortgages, bankruptcies, foreclosures? After watching what our parents and their friends went through, it's no wonder we'd rather rent. And even now, when we want to buy, we can't find a house we can afford!

▪ *Church.* From the numerous scandals in the Catholic Church to the downfall of a number of well-known evangelical leaders, the church as an institution has lost a lot of credibility and moral high ground. And on a personal level, young adults have witnessed church splits, petty politics, and a lack of impact in the community. Meanwhile nonprofits, charities, and causes are tackling real problems and coming up with real solutions. Young adults seem to be going where the action is.

▪ *Pension.* What pension? Companies and governments are cutting pensions left and right, loyalty is no longer rewarded, and nothing is guaranteed. It seems better to gamble on a tech start-up and perhaps become a millionaire in your twenties than to work at a place for decades like your parents did, getting rewarded for years of hard work with not a promotion or a pension but a layoff.

▪ *American Dream.* The suburbs are not our dream destination. Retirement is not exciting, nor does it seem attainable. And even if we've seen our parents or grandparents accomplish the American Dream, many of their achievements appear empty. There must be more to life than a big house and a 401(k).

Millennials have turned this pattern on its head.

Millennials now want to have the discussion in the following order: passion, purpose, *and then* provision. They want to think about the personal, the spiritual, and then—and only then—the professional.

Gen Xers and baby boomers prioritize provision questions above questions of passion and purpose.

Millennials do the opposite.

Before deciding how they will provide for themselves, millennials are first trying to figure out what they are passionate about and what their purpose in life is.

Only then—when the passion and purpose questions have been answered—will millennials move on to questions of provision. They will not discuss how they are going to provide for themselves until they have discovered what is worth (in their opinion) providing.

Now, my generation and I need to take ownership of our part. Ed Cole, founder of the Christian Men's Network, once said, "Maturity doesn't come by age, but rather, acceptance of responsibility." What my generation needs to accept responsibility for is that we're really bad at swinging the pendulum so far from our parents' way of life. And that's not the right outlook either. A life motivated only by provision is empty. Yes. But a life motivated only by passion and purpose is impossible. It's just not how the world works. It's why millennials are job hopping. We want our dream job first. But no famous actor, no great musician, and no successful entrepreneur ever started where they are now. They started at the bottom, doing what they loathed so they could one day do what they love. Before David was a king, he was a shepherd. Before Joseph was in the palace, he was in a prison (how some young people view their current job). I've come to realize that the process enhances the final product. Remind us that it's working under Potiphar that prepared Joseph to work with Pharaoh. Because then we see the process is part of the plan.

> A life motivated only by provision is empty. But a life motivated only by passion and purpose is impossible.

It's critical to understand the flow to this pattern, because it is fundamentally new to American society. And what could happen, and what in my opinion *is* happening, is that young people are shutting their parents out of the planning process for their future. That's what Neil does with his dad. He goes behind his back because he no longer sees his dad looking out for his best interest.

We don't want a generation that's simply repeating or responding to the mistakes of its forefathers. Ideally, we should be learning and expanding on the foundation given to us. As we go forward, I'm going to discuss how to get us back on the same page.

Passionate but Poor

Choosing a job is a lot harder when you're considering the amount of impact you'll make rather than just the amount of money you'll make. It's easy to measure salary. It's hard to measure impact. But studies show young people are choosing their work differently. Fifty-eight percent of millennials report they would take a drastic pay cut if they could have a job that made a difference in the world.[8] This means the metric for choosing a career is no longer the money; it's the calling. It's no longer provision; it's passion and purpose.

The trouble, however, is that the parents of millennials don't realize this shift has taken place and continue to place provision questions ahead of questions of passion and purpose. To the millennial, this is the unforgivable sin. What older generations call pursuing the American Dream we perceive as a millennial nightmare, yet the baffled older generations look at millennials and think our desire for passion and purpose is nothing but a pipe dream!

Here is a question I ask millennials often: "When was the last time your parents expressed concern over your lack of money in the bank or from your job?"

Typically, the answer comes back fast and furious: "All the time! It's one of the main reasons they call anymore."

Sometimes it feels like parents don't really care what you do, as long as it makes money. Doctor, lawyer, engineer, architect. Any of these will suffice. Heaven forbid God calls you to something that doesn't make good money. (Like he did his Son.)

When I started out in ministry, I took every odd job I could to stay afloat and pay my bills. During this period, my father would call me every week, worried about my financial situation. His calls, by the way, were definitely warranted, as there were many weeks I had next to nothing in my checking account. I was living paycheck to paycheck and making do sometimes with about twenty bucks a week for food and drink. I know people in other parts of the world live on far less, but in America twenty dollars doesn't go very far.

My father would say, "Grant, why don't you just get a regular job? You've been approached by multiple companies or churches wanting to hire you. You could have full-time pay and health benefits. You don't have to live like this."

It wasn't an unreasonable position for him to take. But all I could think about was that in taking a job that I wasn't passionate about, I would be trading forty hours (at minimum) of my week to do something that might swell my bank account but not my heart. I would die inside. My provision would be met but not my passions or my purpose.

For me, that was a deal breaker.

One day I told him how I felt. "Dad, you know I've been trying to get Initiative (the nonprofit I started) off the ground for a year now. But every time we talk, you bring up money as if I don't care about it. I've been keeping track. There hasn't been a single phone call in the past year when you didn't at some point bring up the subject of money."

My father was unfazed. *I'm looking after you* was his sentiment. And he was. I thank God for that. And for him. He loves me and he wanted only what was best for me. He was first and foremost concerned about my provision and didn't want to discuss my passion or purpose until my provision had been taken care of. I now understand that his concern for my provision was his way of communicating care, through his generation's worldview. But what I was focused on during that season was my passion and purpose. I was doing enough in the provision department by way of odd jobs, but I wasn't going to do any more than that. I needed to get Initiative off the ground, and I had no dependents leaning on me for food or shelter. Consequently, I was going to do everything in my power to live into my dream and subsist on the bare minimum. I was willing to suffer in the short term for a chance to do what I love in the long run.

I needed my father to trust me while I did this, but he needed to know my provision was taken care of. It makes perfect sense, but I couldn't understand his concern at the time because his refusal to ask about my passion and purpose was all I could focus on. So it didn't matter what he was saying, because all I could hear was what he was not saying.

It would have made a world of difference if my father had at least asked why I was so willing to suffer temporarily. He thoroughly knew my finances, but he didn't thoroughly know my motivation. God, in all his humor, gave me a seemingly reckless vision and a CPA as a father. We were destined for tension. Thanks, God.

Today, by the grace of God, Initiative is alive and well because men and women (my parents' and grandparents' age) believe in what we are doing and give graciously to our cause. We couldn't do what we do without them. Consequently, my father rarely asks me about money these days. He knows I have enough to eat and my bills are paid. But what he still doesn't know well is why I've chosen this life. There is no way he could stand up in front of a crowd of people and in detail tell them why I do what I do. He knows what I do but not why I do it. It's not because he doesn't care. He does. He cares a lot. His primary concern, however, is my provision. Now that my provision is secure, he believes his central duty as a parent has come to an end. He still does not understand that as a Christian, I must go where God calls me, even when that call takes me beyond the boundaries of status quo or what is safe and smart.

John R. Mott, through the Student Volunteer Movement in the late 1880s and '90s, mobilized thousands of young people to the mission field. He wrote a book called *The Evangelization of the World in This Generation*, the title of which became a popular term and goal for young leaders of his time. He even won a Nobel Peace Prize for his work! However, he had some hard words when it comes to letting young people listen to God, even

> "The number one obstacle to world evangelization is Christian parents."
> —JOHN MOTT

when God calls them to do hard things. Before he died, John Mott said, "The number one obstacle to world evangelization is Christian parents."

Christian parents. Wow. Not what I was expecting. But I see how he could get there. A father once told me, "Grant, my worst fears have happened. My daughter loves Jesus so much that she wants to be a missionary." He was joking, but there was a little half-truth in there. It's scary when the child you love is called to be a lamb among wolves—a light in a dark place. But the kingdom needs them. And remember, the King protects them.

There's one sermon on the American Dream that countless millennials and Gen Xers can quote from. It's known as "The Seashells Sermon." It was given by John Piper at the Passion Conference in 2000. The message challenged the American Dream, questioning the goal of retirement in light of eternity, and forty thousand young people left that conference inspired not to waste their lives pursuing the wrong goal. You have to watch it.

▶ Chapter 3, "The Seashells Sermon"

Look, I see enough men and women around me with huge bank accounts who are miserable. Other millennials see it too, and we refuse to walk this path. We don't want to gain the world only to lose our souls. For millennials, losing our souls looks like this: we make money, but we don't make a difference. If you're looking for one sentence to summarize the passion, purpose, and provision discussion, that's it. Our parents want us to make money and then consider making a difference, but we don't want to make money *unless* we are making a difference.

> For millennials, losing our souls looks like this: we make money, but we don't make a difference.

So we understand what millennials want and why there is a generation gap. Now we need to look at what can be done about it.

Questions to Ask

Before reading any further, answer the following questions.

If your millennial son or daughter could provide for himself or herself in the ideal manner, what would that look like? Write down a few of your hopes. Would they be debt free? Would they have a "respectable" job? A healthy 401(k)? A pension? What exactly would it look like for your son or daughter to provide for themselves in the ways you want them to?

1.

2.

3.

Okay, now look back over what you wrote down. And then answer this question: What if they earned everything on this list by a multiple of three, but they didn't live a life aligned with their passions and purpose?

What if they were provided for beyond your wildest dreams, but they never got to exercise their God-given passions or fulfill their God-given purpose? Would you be happy for them?

They'd have a roof over their head and all their bills paid. They'd just feel like something was missing inside. I speak to a lot of parents, and I have yet to hear a parent answer that last question in the affirmative, because while parents want provision for their children, they also want them to keep their souls. However, most young people feel their parents' concern only when it pertains to provision.

So . . . what if parents simply reversed the order of the conversation? Parents can remain concerned about provision but just ask the questions in a different order. Instead of leading the conversation with money, start instead with these questions on passion.

PASSION: WHAT I LOVE TO DO

1. What makes you feel alive?
2. What job would you take a drastic pay cut for?
3. What could you talk about for hours?
4. What subjects did you enjoy most in school?
5. What have you done in your life that you're really proud of?
6. What makes you different?
7. What bothers you when you see it done poorly?
8. What problems or injustices break your heart?
9. What are the top three values you look for in a friend?
10. What do you know well enough to teach others?
11. What qualities do you possess that you are really proud of?
12. Who is doing something you want to do with your life?
13. When do you feel most like yourself?
14. What project or subject could you get lost in for hours without even noticing?
15. What did you love doing as a child?

Then move on to questions of purpose.

PURPOSE: WHAT I WAS MADE TO DO

1. What are you naturally good at?
2. If you got to watch your funeral, what would you want friends and family to say about your character?
3. What system do you want to change?
4. What are some challenges you've overcome in your story?
5. What characters in the Bible do you connect with most, and why?
6. What do people most often ask you for help with?
7. What kind of husband or wife do you want to be?
8. What kind of father or mother do you want to be?
9. If you could share a message with the world, what would you say?

10. What group of people do you like to serve who are often forgotten or neglected?
11. If this was your last year to live, what would you do for yourself, your friends, your family, and the world?
12. What wrong do you want to right?
13. What do people often think you should do for a living?
14. What one word do you want the world to think of when they think of you?
15. If you could start fresh with your life and career, what would you do differently?

Once these questions of passion and purpose have been discussed, feel free to move into questions of provision.

PROVISION: WHAT I NEED TO DO

1. What sacrifices will you have to make?
2. What extra time will you have to give?
3. What kind of mentors will you need to seek?
4. What kind of friends will you need to surround yourself with?
5. What kind of friends will you need to avoid?
6. What time wasters will you have to cut?
7. What is the minimum salary you can live with?
8. What education will you have to pursue?
9. What habits will you have to break?
10. What habits will you have to form?
11. Do you have enough savings to live for six months during a job transition or in pursuit of your passion?
12. Would you be willing to downsize your lifestyle?
13. How much money will you need to earn if you have to pay off college debt?
14. What books or podcasts would you need to invest in?
15. Would you be willing to make a five year plan to accomplish your purpose?

Once these questions have been asked, answered, and discussed, millennials will be far more amenable to conversations about provision. Remember, it's not that they don't want or need to talk about money but that they will be far more receptive to a discussion on provision if they see it as a means to their passion and purpose.

Before I finish this chapter, I want to point out something and I want to thank you for something. Here it is: Millennials get the privilege to consider passion and purpose in their work *because* our parents and grandparents did whatever it took to provide a better life for their kids. If you've never heard a young person say it, thank you. Lord knows no one was coming out of the Great Depression considering their passion or purpose in their work. They just did whatever was necessary to put food on the table! But after decades of faithfulness and sacrifice, this generation has opportunities past generations haven't had, and I'd hate for us to miss them simply because we don't understand each other.

I wish all millennials understood this and felt this way. But they don't. You know that. I know that. There are a few unicorns here and there. But there are a ton of millennials who feed the stereotype. So what do we do with them? Well, keep reading.

Supporting versus Subsidizing

Recently, I spoke to a large gathering of business leaders at Texas Instruments, an event I was pretty excited about because Texas Instruments basically helped my entire generation pass algebra. The questions folks asked were the standard ones concerning how to motivate millennials in the workplace. Finally, somebody stood up and asked the question that was really on everyone's mind. A father asked, "So I hear what you're saying . . . but . . . what do I do if the only thing my son seems to be passionate about is video games?"

The audience burst into laughter. Obviously, the question

struck a nerve. The real question was, "Do I just get behind any-thing my child seems to be passionate about?" The answer is no. I'm not advocating that whatever a young adult is passionate about, they should pursue as a career. Because some young people aren't passionate *enough*. Real passion always spills into provision. If you take the time to have the passion and purpose conversation before the provision conversation, but your child is still unwilling to invest the appropriate time and sacrifice necessary, then it's okay to draw a line. Living into one's passion and purpose takes grit. It takes sacrifice. There is no way around it. If your millennial is unwilling to work for what they want or is too lazy to even figure out what they want, then you have every right to take drastic actions, such as cutting them off financially. Supporting them emotionally does not have to mean subsidizing them financially.

One of the hardest things that ever happened to me was when I dropped out of college and my dad refused to let me move back home. He put my stuff outside the house. When he did that, I was pretty mad. Like, really mad. But I also realized there were real consequences to my decisions. Deep down, I knew this didn't mean my dad didn't care about me. He just wasn't going to ena-ble me.

It sobered me up. Fast.

I knew I needed to choose my next move wisely. I couldn't just do whatever I wanted. I needed money for food and a roof over my head. This made me rely on the Lord like never before. During that season of my life, I memorized Proverbs 3 because I didn't have much direction and I needed to be reminded of the Lord's good-ness. I especially needed to remember Proverbs 3:11–12: "My son, do not despise the Lord's discipline, and do not resent his rebuke, because the Lord disciplines those he loves, as a father the son he delights in."

It was the first time I'd ever memorized an entire chapter of the Bible. It got me thinking. Would I have memorized Scripture and relied on the Lord if I hadn't found myself in a season of weak-ness and need?

This was one of the worst, best seasons of my life. You know, the kind of season you don't want to go back to, but you also don't want to remove from your story? In my weakness, I learned dependence. One of my favorite communicators to my generation, Jonathan Pokluda, says, "If dependence is the goal, then weakness is our advantage." In that season, I learned the advantages of weakness and the power of dependence.

No Obstacle Too Big

There is nothing easy about fighting to do what you feel called to do in life. If a person wants to pursue their passion and find their purpose, then they have no choice but to do the hard work it takes to find it.

A lot of people believe millennials aren't willing to do this hard work because we are lazy or self-absorbed. But millennials aren't any different than generations before us when it comes to laziness, entitlement, and selfishness. Young people have always been hit with these critiques. Elspeth Reeve points out in a brilliant article in *The Atlantic* that in 1976 the *New York Times* said of boomers, "The now generation has now become the ME generation." Sounds like millennials. In 1990, *Time* magazine said of Xers, "They have trouble making decisions. They would rather hike in the Himalayas than climb a corporate ladder. They crave entertainment, but their attention span is as short as one zap of a TV dial."[9]

> Greater than millennials' fear of commitment is our fear of *missing out.*

Is it possible that young people just tend to be more selfish or lazy until they're married with kids? What a lot of people are interpreting as laziness is actually something else. I've found that most millennials aren't lazy. They're just uninspired. People say millennials won't commit to a job. I think they won't compromise for one. If you're selling a dream that sounds like a nightmare, no, we're not going to bite. But sell us a future that fulfills our purpose, and it won't matter how many obstacles are in the way. We'll work for it. People point out that millennials fear commitment. It's true. But I've found there's something we fear even more. Greater than millennials' fear of commitment is our fear of *missing out*. We call it FOMO. Companies that are selling passion-filled work are leveraging FOMO to their advantage. It's a great motivator—far, far greater than guilt.

When a young person finds their passion, no obstacle is too big. Passion will change a person. We see this all the time in a relational way. I've seen teenage boys with the dirtiest rooms and the worst hygiene change in a matter of seconds. Their room and car are suddenly spotless, and their clothes are actually clean. Why? Because a girl is coming over. But not just any girl, *the* girl they're passionate about. When you find your passion, you can get lost for hours in your work. Even if the work is meticulous and mundane, it's like a puzzle to you. It's a game. Any other thing would have lost your attention at the first sign of difficulty, but not your passion. The great thing about finding your passion is that grit doesn't feel like grit. It just feels like a fun part of the process. It doesn't really feel like work. Passion turns careers into callings. Callings turn work into worship.

DEPENDENTS OR DISCIPLES?

I was speaking to a group of Christian business owners recently, a bunch of real go-getters. Men and women who have worked hard to get where they are in life. What's great about Christian business leaders is they tend to understand that success without significance is empty. But what's ironic about this group is that they still want to force their kids to submit to the old system, even though they know it's bankrupt.

So I pointed out to the group that they discovered the importance of significance in their work as a midlife crisis, but young adults are searching for it in a quarter-life crisis. Or in the words of my friend Paul Sohn, a "quarter-life calling." The only difference is that the older generation gets praised for it, while the younger generation gets criticized.

My dad got on me *so much* when I was younger for living irresponsibly. But you know what my parents are doing now? You'll never believe it. They sold the house my brothers and I grew up in, bought an RV, and now they just travel America. What! *Who are these people?* Depending on the season, you can find them at an RV park in Florida, Oregon, California, or Kansas. They work easy odd jobs that pay low wages, because they don't need much. Their costs are so low.

I joke with them that they are now the irresponsible ones living the millennial dream, and I'm now the responsible one showing up to work every day. Once my dad even needed to borrow money from me! (Oh how the tables have turned!) The funny thing is, when I tell older people what my parents are up to now, they think it's so cool! Almost like they're jealous that my parents took the dive.

I have to give it to my parents. There's a freedom they live in now. Once my brothers and I moved out, they really had to consider what they wanted to do with their lives other than just make money. It's a good question, a necessary question. I just don't think my generation wants to wait till the end of their lives to ask it. They're asking it right now.

One of the best encouragements I've gotten from the marketplace community involves a father and son. When I was finished speaking to the Christian business leaders, a man with a huge smile said, "Hey! I have to tell you something I think you'll like."

"Awesome! What's up?" I said.

"I was just going down the elevator. It was full of people, and there was this Asian man in a suit apologizing to his son over the phone for never talking to him about his passion and purpose. So I just want you to know your message really connected today."

What I love about that story is that the father took immediate action, and he did it with full humility. He cared more about that conversation with his son than he cared about the opinion of the other leaders in the elevator. This is huge! Men tend to struggle at admitting their mistakes. Doing so, however, is so powerful. They become unforgettable moments for many young people I know. And I have a feeling that the ending to that father-son story was a happier one than that of *Dead Poets Society*.

▶ Chapter 3, "The Tension between Passion and Provision"

It's never too late to earn your place back at the table in your child's life. Let them explore questions of passion, purpose, and provision while you listen and encourage them. And don't forget that their struggle with these questions is what will most likely lead them to Jesus and his plan for their life.

How many millennials are prepared for the real world? Not many. Does that mean parents should swoop in and rescue them? Not necessarily. Instead parents should point them to Jesus, showing them how to find their confidence in God in the midst of their difficulties. Remember, one man builds his house on the sand of his own wisdom, while the other builds his house on the rock of Christ. Neither house gets to avoid the storm. But one house does survive it. The storm reveals which foundation is more powerful and worthy. When parents step in and save their kids, God's power isn't seen or cherished.

> Our plans and God's plans don't always line up, but maturity happens when we trust his ways more than our wants.

God doesn't wish for our suffering, but God will always make use of it. Our plans and God's plans don't always line up, but maturity happens when we trust his ways more than our wants. Sometimes young people need to suffer. For parents this is painful, but you must remember we have a God who intimately knows our suffering. He shows up in our weaknesses. It's while walking through the valley of the shadow of death that we fear no evil, because God is with us. His rod and his staff, they comfort us. God doesn't just help us in our valleys. He joins us in them.

Think about this: what have been your closest seasons with God? The reality is our most intimate seasons with the Lord most likely began with our most desperate seasons "alone." But we try to rescue young people from desperate seasons. You never want your kids to think, "Though I walk through the valley of the shadow of death, I will fear no evil, for Mom is with me, her purse and her help, they comfort me." Instead of showing your kids how to be disciples of Jesus, you're showing them how to be dependent on you. When you step in to rescue your kids, you might be saving them from the Savior. In the words of Elisabeth Elliot, "God will not protect you from anything that will make you more like Jesus." So why would we? Is it possible that we're trying to protect our kids from something that will make them more like Christ?

> Don't save your kids from the Savior.

Instead help them cultivate their passions, discover their purpose, and labor through the grit of provision.

CHAPTER 4

THE CHURCH'S
REAL PROBLEM

The church doesn't have a millennial problem. It has a discipleship problem.

That's far more serious, because how do you fix a discipleship problem?

Well, the problem is serious but the answer is simple. You fix a discipleship problem by making Jesus' last words our first priority.

So what were his last words? I'm so glad you asked.

What's known as the Great Commission were Jesus' last words. I know there is a lot of talk these days about making America great again. But what Christians need to do is *make the commission great again*. See what I did there? (I may or may not have a red hat with this on it.)

Just before Jesus ascended to the Father, he left explicit instructions for what we, as his followers (aka the church), are supposed to be all about. "Jesus came to them and said, 'All authority in heaven and on earth has been given to me. Therefore go and make disciples of all nations, baptizing them in the name of the Father and of the Son and of the Holy Spirit, and teaching them to obey everything I have commanded you. And surely I am with you always, to the very end of the age'" (Matt. 28:18–20).

The church, then, has one mission: to make disciples of Jesus Christ.

That's it. Making disciples is the core of what the church needs to be about. I believe it's our failure to do this that has turned millennials off from the church. It's not because the church played the wrong music or the pastor didn't wear skinny jeans or have a big enough following on social media. It's because the church stopped taking discipleship seriously. Instead of inviting young people to the same exciting and demanding adventure Jesus called the disciples to, we invited them to join a club and maintain the status quo.

This is why I am not going to give you tips and tricks on how to get millennials back in church. In response to the millennial exodus, blogs and books have dedicated a massive amount of time and energy to describing changes the church can make to win millennials back.

Change the music. Change the venue. Change the name. The details are always different, but the philosophy is the same. Churches just need to make some updates to look and feel relevant to young people. Then young people will come back. There is some truth to this thinking. But here's the deal. Most of it is superficial, time-stamped techniques that might be semi-effective for some young people today but won't be for young people tomorrow. And it definitely won't be relevant for Generation Z, which is coming up behind millennials. Trends are forever changing. That's why they're called trends.

> Instead of calling young people to a demanding adventure, we invited them to join a club.

One of my best friends was saved through the "bus ministries" that were popular in the eighties. Some well-meaning guy would drive a church-owned bus around the neighborhood, hand out candy, and come back Sunday to take the kids to church. Can you imagine somebody trying that today? Someone would call the cops. And rightfully so! Today that ministry sounds like the beginning of a scary movie, but back then it worked. If there is one thing that remains constant in the church, it's that the trends do nothing *but* change.

Billy Graham said, "The methods change, but the message always stays the same."

And he's right. So I don't want to give you tips and tricks when I don't think they're going to be relevant in five to ten years. I want to give you the closest thing we've got to a silver bullet. It will be effective today and every day until Jesus comes back.

It's the one method that will never change because it's the one method given for the message. The method simply is this: Go and make disciples.

I once had a mentor tell me that your sweet spot of influence is among people ten years older than you and ten years younger than you. That's who you relate to best because you understand the times they grew up in. Well, if that's true, then if I disciple someone who disciples someone who disciples someone, then the gospel will influence generation after generation.

> We need to stop treating the Great Commission like the great suggestion.

I believe once we stop treating this like a great suggestion and start trusting it like the Great Commission, revival is just around the corner.

What Discipleship Is Not

So what is discipleship? And what does it look like? Well, before we can understand what discipleship is and how we can go about doing it together, we first need to talk about what it is not. So let's do that now.

DISCIPLESHIP IS NOT A CLASSROOM

Churches focus too much on Bible studies, Sunday school classes, and sermons. Yeah, I just said that. Look, these are all great things.

Christians have always taken learning seriously, and we shouldn't stop now. We need to be instructed in the ways of our faith if we are to grow in our faith. But traditional didactic activities in and of themselves, while helpful, are not adequate for discipleship.

We cannot expect Christians to become like Jesus if all we ever ask of them is to come to classes, sit in pews, and remain quiet while someone else teaches them about Jesus. Listening to pastors and priests and teachers will always be a part of the Christian journey. No doubt about it. After all, Jesus did a lot of teaching. It's just not the *only* thing he did. The vast majority of the teachings of Jesus were not delivered in so-called sermons. They were just things he said to the disciples along the way—things they never would have heard if they hadn't been following him in his life. Formal education is good. But education is not enough.

In the Greek, the literal meaning of *discipleship* is "being a student." But to understand this properly, we have to understand that being a student in the ancient world was very different than it is today. Today a student shows up for a class at a particular location at a particular time. But in the ancient world, a student hung on every word his teacher said at all times of the day. Students followed their teacher everywhere, slept outside his door at night, and tried to do much more than simply learn facts from him. They tried to become like him. This was a 24/7 thing.

I had heart surgery when I was born. It was crazy abrupt and crazy expensive. I can't imagine how difficult it was for my parents. It's scary enough when you have your first child. *Am I ready? Do I have what it takes?* But how much more nerve-racking when your firstborn enters the world and you need to rush him into surgery!

Now, if my parents got to choose between a doctor who's closely read one hundred books on heart surgeries or a doctor who's closely watched one hundred heart surgeries, who do you think they'd pick? (Not to mention that discipleship is *assisting* in the work of the disciple maker.)

Discipleship is more than the transfer of information. It's the transformation of a person through following.

DISCIPLESHIP IS NOT MENTORING

Discipleship is more than mentorship. Meeting for coffee once a month is a great thing for mentors and mentees to do, but it's not as robust as full-blown discipleship. The church has fallen into a bad habit of equating discipleship with meeting over an early morning coffee to pray, read the Bible, and talk a little bit about life. This is beneficial, but it's not really discipleship.

Jesus didn't set a time to meet with his disciples for a brief conversation once a week for three years. Discipleship wasn't something he took care of before going about his business. Discipleship *was* his business.

Here is a critical distinction:

The church can no longer bank on just providing content and a message as their main commodity, because my generation can google content all day. The value of content is at an all-time low in this digital world. This is impacting colleges, the publishing industry, and even the church. You don't *need* to go to church to get content. Millennials can live-stream a message, download a podcast, or watch a YouTube video, but there's still no app for genuine connection and life-on-life discipleship. That's what the church can provide that the world can't.

Now, when it comes to mentorship and discipleship, there is a massive difference between scheduling time to meet versus inviting someone in. Mentorship says, "Add me to your calendar." Discipleship says, "Include me in your calendar." Later, I'll dive into the mechanics of how this can be done. For now, just remember that discipleship > mentorship. Mentorship is good. Discipleship is great.

The apostle Paul told the Thessalonians, "Because we loved you so much, we were delighted to share with you not only the gospel of God but our lives as well" (1 Thess. 2:8). Which do you think is more impactful: when you tell someone the gospel with your mouth, or when you show it to them with your life?

My friend Connor perfectly illustrated this "follow me" mindset of discipleship a few years back, when he asked the president of Dallas Baptist University, Dr. Adam Wright, to disciple him. As you can imagine, Dr. Wright is a wildly busy guy. But when Connor approached Adam and asked, Adam agreed even though he had no spare time to give. Adam did,

> Discipleship isn't adding something to your calendar. It's including someone in your calendar.

however, say he needed to wait a semester before taking on Connor as a disciple, because he was already discipling three other guys, meeting with each of them once a week for thirty minutes. But Connor told him, "I'm actually not interested in doing *that* kind of discipleship. I don't want to meet with you. I want to follow you." Connor then explained that he was asking Adam if he could follow him in his work life, church life, family life, or personal life.

Adam was a little taken aback, but once he realized that

Connor's proposal was not going to cost him any more time, he accepted. Connor wasn't asking for his time; Connor was simply asking for his availability. So they agreed and got down to it.

Fast-forward a few months. It's six in the morning, and Adam is preparing for the coming rigorous day by faithfully executing his early morning routine of praying, studying the Word, jogging, and eating breakfast with his wife and kids before driving to work.

And guess who is doing it right alongside him?

Connor.

When Connor asked Adam how he prepared for the morning, Adam described his routine and then invited Connor to spend the night at his house so he could do it with him. "Aren't you supposed to be following me?" he said.

So that's what Connor did. He texted me the first time he followed Adam in his morning routine. "Bro . . . get ready to feast your eyes on a new man. I am going to wake up early every single day!"

How awesome is it when a young person's passion is guided by older people's wisdom?

Think about how Connor was affected by participating in Adam's example as opposed to just hearing about it over coffee in a mentoring relationship? Great leaders wake up early. That's no secret. We've all heard that. Adam could have told Connor an early morning routine is crucial. But seeing it makes a huge difference. Something extraordinary happens when discipline and habits are caught more than they are taught. When they are caught through experience, you get to feel the benefits of rising early, entering into the presence of God, and accomplishing something, all while the rest of the world is just waking up.

These are the kinds of moments that mature young people. When a young person begins to change their habits in productive ways and envision where their life might be in five years if they practiced their new habits every day, things really start cooking. Connor began asking himself, "What would it take for me to become a man like Adam Wright?" He had at least one answer by way of example: wake up early and start with God.

Discipleship is always better caught than taught.

The disciples never would have been prepared to do what God needed them to do if they'd just sat around and met with Jesus. They needed to *follow* him. Almost every story we have of Jesus with the disciples is of them on the move. They are always going somewhere with him. And it's there, along the way, that they learn. The earliest Christians were called Followers of the Way. We too are followers of the Way—followers of Christ.

Mentorship is good.

Discipleship is great, just like the commission.

DISCIPLESHIP IS NOT A SMALL GROUP

Small groups have become too popular in the church. Now, before you accuse me of heresy and throw this book in the trash, hear me out. I'm not saying small groups are bad. What I *am* saying is that the church's love of small groups has become a problem.

Think of it this way. You often hear people quote the Bible as saying that money is the root of all evil. But the Bible doesn't actually say that. We all know money can be used for good or bad in this world. What the Bible says is, "the love of money is a root of all kinds of evil" (1 Tim. 6:10). It's the same with small groups. Small groups aren't bad, but our love of them frustrates me.

Why? Because I think it's our cop-out for discipleship. Small groups are easier to manage than discipleship, so they've become our acceptable replacement. There's a popular saying in the church: "Circles are better than rows." I agree. But do you know what's even better than circles?

Disciples.

When I consult with churches, I almost always ask the pastor the following question: "If I were a new Christian at your church, where would I get discipled?"

About 90 percent of the pastors say in a small group. Again, small groups aren't bad, but if that is the extent of the plan for discipleship, then Houston, we have a problem.

And most of the time, it is the plan. Most pastors admit

that other than small groups, their church doesn't really have a concrete plan of action for creating new disciples. When I press them further on the issue, asking, "Why not?" they often say they believe discipleship needs to develop *organically* in a small group context.

Organic discipleship? I'm not trying to be obnoxious, but I honestly don't know what that even means.

Whenever I'm unsure about a proposed church strategy, I try to view it through the lens of the Great Commission.

> Circles are better than rows. And disciples are better than circles.

Let's look again at what Jesus said: "Go and make disciples of all nations, baptizing them in the name of the Father and of the Son and of the Holy Spirit, and teaching them to obey everything I have commanded you" (Matt. 28:18–20).

THE FOUR CALLS TO ACTION

Okay, so there are four actions Jesus calls us to in the Great Commission. Let's take each one in turn and ask ourselves whether it's wise to have an organic approach to accomplishing that task.

1. GO

If I show up at church and ask to be involved in missions—if I ask to go—I will be told exactly what to do. There will be a mission and outreach team for me to contact. There will be mission trips I can sign up for. There might even be a list of local nonprofits the church partners with to serve the community. If I am mission minded, the church will provide a place for me to go and people to go with. No church I know of leaves missions to develop organically. There is a path. There is a team. There is a plan. Always. We don't just expect people to figure it out and plan their own trips across the globe. We strategically guide them to well-vetted partners.

2. BAPTIZE

If I show up at church and ask to be baptized, I will be told exactly what to do. Imagine the following scenario playing out in your church. A new Christian approaches your pastor and informs him that she has just been saved by Jesus and wants to be baptized. Your pastor says, "That's great news! Let me know how that goes."

No way. That would never happen. You would be concerned if your pastor did that! Baptism is what the church does. It will look different in every church, but the path to baptism will be carefully laid out. The church does not wait for baptism to be done organically in local lakes, rivers, and Jacuzzis. It strategically guides people through the process.

3. TEACH

If I show up at church and tell the pastor I want to learn about Jesus and Christianity, the most detailed plan will be offered. I'll be told about classes, sermon series, blogs, books, conferences, retreats. Teaching is so highly valued in the church that most churches spend a good amount of their time planning what is to be taught. The teaching pastor is often allocated numerous hours for sermon prep. I have never known a church to leave teaching open to whoever is organically feeling it that Sunday. I have never shown up on Sunday morning at a church that didn't have a strategic plan for what was going to be taught.

4. MAKE DISCIPLES

If I show up at church and tell the pastor I want to get discipled, he or she will most likely tell me to join a small group. Beyond that, there usually isn't much of a plan.

So Jesus tells us to do four primary things in the Great Commission, and it turns out the church is pretty good at executing three of them. You can see the problem. It doesn't make sense to not plan on making disciples. But this is precisely what the church does when its entire approach to discipleship is summed up by the admonition "Go join a small group."

One last time. Small groups aren't bad. They're just not enough. And I don't think they're even first. I think discipleship is. Jesus didn't start a small group and then pick disciples out of it. He picked disciples, and that started a small group.

My ultimate question, then, is this: Why do we approach discipleship so organically when Jesus approached it so strategically? If I put fifty people in your church in separate rooms and tell them, "Write down your church's discipleship strategy," are you confident their answers will be the same? If not, then we haven't properly given our people any language or direction for something Jesus said is high priority. I've found that values without vehicles eventually become just cool words on the wall.

> I've found that values without vehicles eventually become just cool words on the wall.

You know, I'm only half Mexican, and I don't know the language well, but I swear that when churches use the word organic, it's Spanish for "we have absolutely no plan whatsoever."

Just think organic vegetables. It basically means the vegetables are untouched. They haven't been changed, they haven't been altered, and they haven't been tampered with. Well, I'm convinced that when Jesus entered the disciples' lives, they were changed, altered, and tampered with.

I'm not saying discipleship is easy. I'm just saying it's worth it. The Great Commission needs great attention, not organic hopes or spiritual finger-crossing.

I said it before and I'll say it again. We don't have a millennial problem. We have a discipleship problem. And if we don't fix it, then millennials will be the last of our worries. Because there's already another generation on the way. So what we prioritize over the next ten years will make or break the American church.

DISCIPLE OR CHRISTIAN?

The word Christian appears in the New Testament only three times. I bet you didn't know that. I also bet you didn't know this: the word disciple appears 269 times.

Let both of these facts melt your brain for a moment.

As Christians, we believe that every word in the Bible is "God-breathed and is useful for teaching, rebuking, correcting and training in righteousness" (2 Tim. 3:16). This means we know that God intentionally made the word disciple appear 266 more times than he did the word Christian.

The late, great Dallas Willard described this perfectly when he said, "The New Testament is a book about disciples, by disciples, and for disciples of Jesus Christ."

Nonetheless, I think most Christians are slow to describe themselves as disciples of Jesus. Saying that we are Christians is far more comfortable.

Let's look at what discipleship entailed for Jesus.

"While walking by the Sea of Galilee, [Jesus] saw two brothers, Simon (who is called Peter) and Andrew his brother, casting a net into the sea, for they were fishermen. And he said to them, 'Follow me, and I will make you fishers of men'" (Matt. 4:18–19 ESV).

The marks of discipleship come directly from Jesus himself, in three parts.

1. Follow me: Join my life.
2. I will make you: I commit to make you something new.
3. Fishers of men: This can't just terminate with us.

I want to emphasize Jesus' words "I will make you" because it's a commitment.

It's very easy to make fun of young people who are dating, because their relationship status is often so ambiguous these days. They struggle with commitment. This can especially be humorous if you come from a time long, long ago, when you were either in a relationship or you weren't. It was that simple. Binary.

These days, however, if you ask a young couple spending significant time together if they are a thing, you might get any one of the following answers.

- "We're just friends."
- "We're just hanging out."
- "We like each other."
- "We're talking."
- "We're dating."
- "We're waiting."
- "We're tindering."
- "We're courting."

Talk about #DTRprobs. Defining the relationship can be hard for young people. But you know what? I think defining the relationship can be hard for church folk too. People say my generation has fear of commitment. Well, I think Christians have fear of commitment—*the* commitment.

I have found that most Christians consider themselves to be disciples of Jesus Christ, even though they have never committed to disciple someone, like Jesus Christ.

Jesus asked, "Why do you call me, 'Lord, Lord,' and do not do what I say?" (Luke 6:46).

When you say, "I will make you," you're making the kind of commitment often made in some of the greatest stories ever told. It's the tipping point in many well-known epics.

One influential book in Hollywood and the world of literature is *The Hero with a Thousand Faces* by Joseph Campbell. This book informed the storytelling of George Lucas, Stanley Kubrick, Bob Dylan, Walt Disney, and countless others. The basic premise of the book is that every great story starts with the main character experiencing these three events:

■ The Call to Adventure
■ Refusal of the Call
■ Supernatural Aid

Think about a traditional movie plot. It starts with a young man with a dream in his heart. He knows he is different and there is something he must do with his difference, something that will help others. But then he encounters challenges and obstacles that hinder him with feelings of inadequacy. He wants to become who he is meant to be, but his abilities lag behind the call. He needs help.

Enter the sage, a mentor who comes alongside our budding hero to ensure he becomes the hero.

We've seen this over and over again.

Mr. Miyagi and the Karate Kid. Obi-Wan Kenobi and Luke Skywalker. Morpheus and Neo. Professor X and Wolverine. Gandalf and Frodo. Maui and Moana. Tony Stark and Spider-Man.

This "supernatural aid" disrupts the story of the young person but ignites a new story. The sage commits to help the young person, and it changes his life. But I'd also say that the life change is mutual.

I think the Karate Kid also changed Mr. Miyagi's life. I think Frodo changed Gandalf's life.

Discipleship is mutually beneficial.

In the Bible, even before Jesus' time, discipleship was the fundamental pattern for life, especially for the people God used.

Joshua followed Moses.

Elisha followed Elijah.

Ruth followed Naomi.

Solomon followed David.

The list from the Old Testament could go on for a while.

Turn to the New Testament, and you see the same pattern playing itself out.

Timothy followed Paul.

John Mark followed Barnabas.

And before that, the disciples followed Jesus.

The pattern is so simple. Followers of God form followers of God.

But without these necessary interruptions, our lives become predictable, stagnant, even boring.

BAPTIZING BORING

I saw a study a few years back that asked unbelievers about adjectives that best describe Christians. Of course, words like judgmental and hypocritical made the list. But one word hit a chord with me because it was a big reason I didn't want to be a Christian when I was younger.

The Barna Group found that 68 percent of unbelievers would describe Christians as boring.[10]

I can't stand this statistic! Jesus was many things, but boring wasn't one of them.

- Boring people don't have five thousand followers flocking to hear their boring message.
- Boring people don't get approached at weddings to make the party better.
- Boring people don't get crucified for their boring beliefs.
- Boring people aren't greeted with palm branch parades when they enter cities.
- Boring people don't inspire martyrs to give up everything for their boring cause.
- Boring people don't change the world.

My point is this: our God is *not* boring! The world altered its calendar and gauged human history by everything before Christ (BC) and after Christ (AD). His life made a mark. His life made a difference. His life was everything but boring.

So here's my question. If the Christ we follow isn't boring, why in the world are we?

Growing up, I always thought Christians were decently nice people; they were just way too boring. They lacked angst. They lacked a faith that cost them anything. So when I saw this study, I could totally relate. But I think the situation is worse than it looks.

I don't think Christians are just boring. I think Christians are bored.

I think many older Christians were once born-again Christians and now they're just *bored*-again Christians. They're waiting on the next message, conference, or experience that will ignite their faith. All while the Great Commission is at their doorstep. The reality is, we are bored because we are disobedient. I bet painters who don't paint are bored. I bet dancers who don't dance are bored. I bet writers who don't write are bored. And I'm convinced that disciples who don't disciple are bored.

> Many older Christians were once born-again Christians, and now they're just *bored*-again Christians.

It reminded me of a story my friend Chad Hennings told me about his dog named DeSoda. When his kids were very young, he got them a puppy. This puppy, like all puppies, had a ton of energy and lacked a lot of wisdom. DeSoda always tried to run away when the door opened, always tried to jump on any stranger who walked in the home, and always barked obnoxiously. Then a decade went by. DeSoda was now an old dog and no longer a young puppy. His energy was gone. His desire for adventure was gone. Heck, he didn't even care anymore when a stranger walked in the house. He would just lift his head from the mat, give them a nod, and go back to sleep. In dog years, DeSoda was really old. They were pretty sure he was going to die soon.

So the kids, now young teenagers, asked Chad, "Dad! Dad! Can we please get a new dog? *DeSoda is so boring now!* He never plays with us anymore. He just wants to sit around the house all day."

Chad conceded and got them a new puppy. And the process

repeated itself. Their new puppy, Beau, had a ton of energy and no wisdom. Except one difference was, their puppy Beau had DeSoda to show him the way. Beau and DeSoda became really good friends; they were like peas and carrots. All the puppy passion and energy in Beau would get DeSoda to do things he normally wouldn't do. DeSoda was playing outside again. He was modeling for Beau where to go to the bathroom. DeSoda was now wrestling with Beau. He had a renewed energy, and the kids could tell.

Chad told me, "The crazy thing is we thought DeSoda was going to die that year. It just wasn't looking good for him. But he ended up living four more years. And I'm convinced it was because of Beau!" Then he said a profound thing we've all heard before but never in this way. He said, "You may not be able to teach an old dog new tricks, but you can give an old dog a new puppy." I added, "And that new puppy can give an old dog a new *purpose.*"

I just wonder how many old dogs in the church are bored out of their minds, and their lives would be radically changed if they'd just find a young puppy.

I've said it before and I'll say it again. We need each other.

DISCIPLESHIP ISN'T ADDING SOMETHING to your calendar.

JANUARY

COFFEE AT 3PM

IT'S INCLUDING SOMEONE →IN← your calendar.

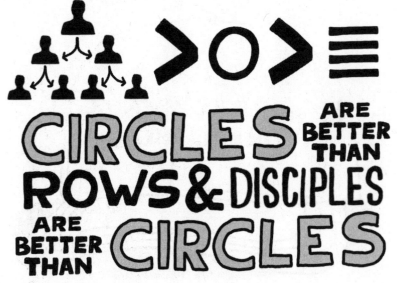

CIRCLES ARE BETTER THAN ROWS & DISCIPLES ARE BETTER THAN CIRCLES

What You Count and What You Celebrate Create Your Culture

Hearing that the church is declining because it has failed in discipleship can be difficult to accept and process. You may be thinking, "So you actually believe millennials are the first generation to not get discipled?" I'll admit: in a way, I used to. Until a pastor from Houston, with tears in his eyes, asked me something that changed my tone. He said, "Grant, I've never realized how much my generation has dropped the ball in discipleship until now. But please try to give us a little grace? Most of my generation wasn't discipled either."

I had never thought about that.

So if discipleship has been neglected for some time now, why is it that my generation, millennials, is being set apart and so thoroughly scrutinized for our differences? Here are some of my thoughts.

It seems that young people haven't changed much. But our culture has changed a ton! We, as the church, for years have been forfeiting our right to disciple the next generation, but now it's finally caught up with us. We've let the world raise our kids, and now we're seeing what David Platt, in the book *Radical*, called "the cost of non-discipleship." Today's culture isn't just different from the church. It's often against it. And perceives us as being against them.

I once heard Tim Keller say to a small group of leaders, "Twenty years ago culture labeled the church as irrelevant. But now culture labels the church as hostile." We have to understand that this generation of Christians has inherited an identity that is at odds with most of their peers. Historically, even if you didn't really love God, it was culturally expected that you went to church and lived a decently moral life. But now if you go to church and try to live a moral life, especially if you stand for biblical values, you're labeled judgmental and closed-minded. We've been allowing culture to disciple our youth for decades; the only difference is that culture isn't on our side anymore. And now we're becoming the minority.

THE TIMES ARE CHANGING

Just to help you wrap your mind around it, here are some major cultural shifts that have happened along the way for millennials. Some have changed entire industries. Some have changed our day-to-day lives. And some would have been straight-up *unfathomable* just thirty years ago.

- CNN launches (1980)
- Apple releases Macintosh (1984)
- Launch of the internet (1991)
- Founding of Amazon (1994)
- Reality TV takes off (1999)
- 9/11 attacks (2001)
- Launch of Facebook (2004)
- Google goes public (2004)
- YouTube makes the world smaller (2005)
- The first iPhone (2007)
- Netflix launches video streaming (2007)

- Airbnb disrupts travel industry (2008)
- Great Recession (2008)
- Uber disrupts travel industry (2009)
- First black president (2009)
- Colorado and Washington legalize weed (2012)
- Mass media attention to police shootings begins (2012)
- #BlackLivesMatter (2013)
- Same-sex marriage legalized (2015)
- Orlando shooting (2016)
- Donald Trump assumes office as president (2017)
- #MeToo movement (2017)

 CHAPTER 5, "THE NUMERIC IMPACT OF CULTURE SHIFTING"

The times are changing, and it's changing everything. But the change that concerns me most is how people see the church. One of the most sobering ways to illustrate this is to get out your computer and search something. Seriously, get out your computer or your phone. You'll be shocked when you see what I'm about to show you. Go back to our old trusty friend yahoo.com and search, "Why are Christians so," and then let Yahoo populate the rest. Do this and don't read more until you do. Try inputting different letters after "Why are Christians so" and see what comes up.

CHAPTER 5, "YAHOO REVEALS ALL"

Okay.

These are sincere questions people are asking in the privacy of their home. This isn't the world trying to criticize the church. This is thousands of people genuinely trying to figure out why.

It's a lot easier to claim God when going to church is socially acceptable. It's a lot harder when saying you're a Christian is immediately associated with everything you must be against. So we're talking about a generation that hasn't been discipled, with a fairly weak faith, who are being sent out as lambs among wolves, but are nowhere near equipped for the persecution coming their way. I think this is why they go to college and fall away in droves. We've influenced them but we haven't discipled them. So let's talk about why millennials have chosen the influence of the culture over the influence of the church.

Millennials haven't rejected the church because it's too exclusive or too traditional. This is what you'll hear on TV or read in blogs. But it's not true. I've said it before and I'll say it again. Millennials have rejected the church for a pretty simple reason: the church has asked too little of them.

What do I mean?

The church has failed to call millennials out of their ordinary lives and into the extraordinary life of Jesus. The church has failed to invite millennials into a great commission. Instead we've settled for just a decent commission. Even our numbers show this. Fifty-one percent of churchgoing Christians say they've never even heard of the Great Commission![11]

Few words today have as much negative connotation as the word millennials. People love making fun of this generation. I mean just Google image search the word millennial, and you'll see hundreds of photos of hipsters on their phone or computer. We don't view them in a positive light. These are the most common adjectives I hear associated with the word millennials:

> Why is the most cause-oriented generation in the world neglecting the most cause-oriented organization in the world, the church?

entitled, noncommittal, transient, narcissistic, impatient. The list can go on and on. But there's one positive description that everyone agrees on. Millennials are cause oriented. They are activists! They're so quick to put an ice bucket on their head, an X on their hand, or even a poster on their wall so they can find Kony. But think about this. Why is the most cause-oriented generation in the world neglecting the most cause-oriented organization in the world, the church?

Because we have taken the greatest cause ever and watered it down to attending an event. Merely showing up Sunday and inviting all your friends is just not that compelling. We have a generation that's basically saying, "Send me, I'll go." And we're replying, "No. Wait. Stay here."

Look at Jesus

If we're going to reach this next generation, we have to change our priorities. And few things adjust my priorities like looking at Jesus. It's one thing to receive him as my Lord and Savior; it's another to respond to him as my role model. If this generation is looking to change the world, let's look at the man who changed the world so much that they altered the calendar around his birth.

Think about this. We have almost no idea what Jesus was up to before he was thirty. Of course, we have his birth. But then what? Outside of one story about him when he was twelve years old and ditched his parents to stay behind in the temple, we have nothing. *Nothing.* In the Gospels, we constantly hear people say, "Isn't that just the carpenter's son?" In other words, "Wait? That guy? For real? That nobody? He's the Messiah?"

Have you ever thought about what that means? It means the Creator of the universe, the one who holds all things together, lived on earth as a man for thirty years, and nobody—to our knowledge—thought twice about it. Mind. Blown. This makes it extremely important to notice *when* people started paying attention to the life of Christ.

So when do they start paying attention? When the Gospels start. When do the Gospels start? When Jesus starts discipling people. Jesus' ministry becomes noteworthy in the Scriptures when he begins making disciples. Before that, we and his community don't know much about him. Moreover, let's consider what he does in the Gospels. He does some pretty incredible things. Here are a few:

- He is born of a virgin.
- He lives a sinless life.
- He miraculously feeds the five thousand.
- He casts out demons.
- He walks on water.
- He heals people.
- He brings people back from the grave.
- He himself comes back from the grave!
- He exchanges his righteousness for our sinfulness.
- He offers salvation for all who will believe.

Now imagine he still does all these incredible things. But imagine the one and only difference is that Jesus doesn't let twelve guys tag along with him while he does them.

How would this change things? Would the church still exist today? Who would have known how to carry on his work? Would the thousands he preached to be ready to go into all the world like the disciples did, even if they were going to be beaten and eventually martyred?

I don't think so. Crowds are fickle. Jesus often had them, but they weren't there in the end. The same crowd that welcomed him on Palm Sunday abandoned him on Good Friday. In John 6, everyone has deserted Jesus, grumbling, "This is a hard teaching. Who can accept it?" But when Jesus looks at the Twelve and asks, "You do not want to leave too, do you?" Peter responds, "Lord, to whom shall we go? You have the words of eternal life. We have come to believe and to know that you are the Holy One of God" (vv. 60, 67–69).

Wow. Good answer! Yet this confidence didn't happen overnight. It didn't happen in one message. It happened over years of following Jesus. What I'm trying to say is I don't know if we'd be standing here today if Jesus hadn't dedicated his ministry to making disciples.

Too Busy with Ministry?

Here's where it gets really crazy. A lot of Christians feel like they aren't able to disciple anyone because they have too much on their plates. I honestly can't tell you how many pastors have told me this. A pastor recently said, "Grant, I really do want to disciple someone, but I'm just way too busy with ministry right now."

Too busy with ministry? What does that even mean?

What the heck is ministry if you're not making disciples? Jesus' ministry begins with him making disciples and ends with him making disciples. His entire ministry hinges on making disciples!

We don't even know about Jesus' ministry until he starts making disciples, and we wouldn't be here to do ministry if he hadn't made disciples. So unless we believe we're more important than Christ or our work is more urgent than his, we have to stop making excuses and start thinking solutions. I don't know who we think we are when we believe we can just read the Bible like discipleship isn't in there.

Ministry is stressful, and pastors are called to meet the needs of so many people. It's insane. I totally get that. Most pastors are honestly doing the best they can on limited budgets and time. But the hard truth is that discipleship is not some hindrance or distraction from ministry. *It is the ministry.* It's the ministry that fuels the other stuff we consider ministry. It's the bedrock. If you're doing "ministry" but you're not doing discipleship, then you're just doing activities. Good activities. Time-consuming activities. Just not ministry. Surely there are pastors out there who are exhausted

> If you're doing "ministry" but you're not doing discipleship, then you're just doing activities.

of feeling like party promoters and event planners. Constantly having to manufacture energy to get people to care about the next event. Surely, there must be leaders out there who feel in their souls, *There's got to be more than this!*

Misleading Metrics

I know I'm coming off strong, but I've seen the misleading metrics of chasing bigger audiences, and it just doesn't amount to much. I live in the ministry mecca of the world, Dallas, Texas. We have more than 4,800 churches in the Dallas–Fort Worth Metroplex. Just to get an idea of how many that is, if I wanted to visit all the churches in my city and went to a different one every Sunday, it'd take me ninety-two years to see them all! We don't just have a lot of churches; we have a lot of big churches. Some of them are the size of airports. This is a city where a church can have around three thousand people and still be referred to as a small church. I'm dead serious. There are churches that have three thousand to five thousand members, and no one's ever heard of them.

My point is this: If getting more people to an event on Sunday is the main objective, shouldn't Dallas be one of the most transformed cities in the world? Shouldn't Dallas look shockingly different than most cities in our nation?

But we don't look different. We look just like every other city, and sometimes even worse. Our mayor announced in 2017 that we have the nation's third-largest disparity gap between the rich and the poor. We are the nation's second most popular hub for human trafficking. Ninety-one percent of Dallas public school students are not graduating college-ready in math and science. Dallas–Fort Worth is the largest recipient of refugees, but most Christians have never been to the Samaria that is their neighborhood. And in 2016, we made the news for the largest police massacre since 9/11 when five officers were gunned down and nine others were injured.

So I'm not saying forsake the gathering. I'm just saying the gathering alone is not the win. If it were, my city should look different.

We must change the scorecard and stop making excuses for why we don't disciple. If our pastors aren't discipling, our people aren't discipling. If our people aren't discipling, our city is without God, and therefore without hope.

Jim Cymbala used to say that most churches measure their

success by "attendance, buildings, and cash. A-B-C: The new holy trinity."[12]

Churches need people, money, and space. I get that. I really do. But.

Jesus had five thousand people following him, far away from their homes, without food, and with no clear idea of where they were heading. And yet they went anyway. They followed because that's how badly they wanted to hear him and learn from him. This wasn't a seeker-sensitive group. This group was hungry to learn more than they were hungry to eat.

But what is even more intriguing and inspiring is not what the masses do but what Jesus does when he gets his largest audience to hear his life-changing message. He doesn't start a megachurch. He doesn't create a conference, and he doesn't launch a podcast. He preaches the Word of God, feeds the people physically, and then jumps on a boat with his disciples to sail away somewhere else!

What was he thinking? Most church leaders today would call that a wasted opportunity. Possibly even foolish. But not Jesus. Jesus wasn't using the same scorecard we use to measure our ministries.

> We see discipleship as a burden. Jesus saw it as the main objective.

We see discipleship as a burden. Jesus saw it as the main objective.

Jesus knew that faith a mile wide but only an inch deep could never compare with a few good men and women who were fully devoted to the cause. Most of us in ministry are focused on building an audience, but Jesus was committed to building an army. It's far easier to build an event people attend than a culture people adhere to.

John Wesley understood this when he said, "Give me one hundred preachers who fear nothing but sin and desire nothing but God, and I care not a straw whether they be clergymen or laymen, [they] alone will shake the gates of hell and set up the kingdom of heaven upon earth."

It's not about the number of people who show up. It's about the number of people who buy in. Remember, what you count and what you celebrate create your culture.

EMPOWERING THE PEOPLE, NOT ONE PASTOR

I've had the privilege of traveling to Israel three times now. It is definitely one of my favorite places on earth. It's such a powerful experience to see the land where Jesus walked and talked and changed the world. It brings the Bible to life in so many ways, and the Jewish culture is so rich. You don't read the Bible the same after you've been to Israel.

In the garden of Gethsemane, I had a particularly powerful experience. As I was standing there taking it in, I noticed a group from Thailand. Then I spotted a group from Uganda. Then I saw a group from Australia. I thought, *Man, people from all over the world are coming to see where my God, Jesus, changed everything.*

That's when it hit me.

Jesus never went to Thailand.

Jesus never went to Uganda.

Jesus never went to Australia.

Then, *Whoa . . . Jesus never went to America!*

But his disciples did.

Jesus changed the world, even though he lived in only one tiny corner of it. He discipled people who discipled people who discipled people, creating an unbroken chain that continues today all around the world.

The great thing about discipleship is that when we start making disciples, we stop relying on the church to feed us. Instead we start relying on the church to launch us. We move away from being a mere member and turn toward being devoted owners. We move from an audience mentality to an army mentality. This is not only what millennials want; it's what they need. It's what we all need.

The irony is that the business world is doing a better job at this than the church is. Here's what I mean.

Do you know what car company has more cars on a global scale than any other?

More cars across the world than Ford?

More cars across the world than Volkswagon?

More cars across the world than Toyota?

> The church doesn't need mere members. It needs devoted owners.

That company would be Uber.

Do you know what company rents more property globally than any other hotel chain?

More properties across the world than Hilton?

More properties across the world than Marriott?

And definitely more properties across the world than Motel 6?

That company would be Airbnb.

You know what's brilliant about their strategies? The companies don't own any of what makes them so powerful and successful. Uber's platform has access to millions of cars globally, but they don't own any of it. Their people do. Airbnb's platform is disrupting the hotel industry, but they don't own any property. Their people do.

These companies are benefiting from the perks of discipleship and multiplication. They haven't just gained an audience of fans. They've raised an army of owners and have thus decentralized leadership. What's beautiful about decentralized leadership structures is that they're not dependent on their charismatic leader for survival. It's the devoted contributors who are the real heart and soul of the operation.

Uber and Airbnb are household names that came out of nowhere and completely changed the cab and hotel game. But can you name their CEOs? I doubt it! I bet even fewer of us know that the original CEO of Uber was recently fired for some pretty awful behavior. Meanwhile, what's happened to the company? It's continued its revolutionary disruption of the transportation industry. Why? Because it's not about one person.

It reminds me of what Jesus said to his disciples: "When I leave, you will do greater things" (John 14:12, my wording). This isn't often the case in the church. How many well-known pastors have stepped down from their church to suddenly find their congregation in shambles?

This is how it usually goes down: A charismatic leader plants a church. The church grows rapidly alongside the reputation of the pastor. Before too long, the pastor is a nationally known writer or speaker who attracts congregants from all over the country—sometimes even from all over the world.

Then the pastor, for whatever reason, leaves the church. It could be a scandal or that it's simply time for him to retire. Regardless of whether the pastor leaves under a cloud of suspicion or departs with trumpets sounding his praise, the results are often the same.

The church splits into different camps. Satellite campuses begin to struggle. The overall attendance shrinks. Resources plummet. And you know what happens from there. Church morale is gone and some of the satellite campuses have no choice but to shut their doors and close the operation. The pain and carnage are far flung and widely felt.

This is not the model Jesus gave us for church. He gave us a model that lasts.

A charismatic leader is good, but discipleship is great. One has a shelf life. The other is timeless.

A charismatic leader is good, but discipleship is great. One has a shelf life. The other is timeless.

Is it possible that we're celebrating the wrong gift in the church? Everyone wants to be a great communicator. But few want to be great disciple makers. Let us never forget that after only three years, Jesus' model of ministry went on to grow without him.

WE MEASURE WHAT WE VALUE MOST

To understand more about where the church has fallen short, let's take another lesson from the corporate world. Every successful company measures the products they create and sell. If they didn't do this, they would cease to exist. Nike measures shoes. Tesla measures cars. Chick-fil-A measures sandwiches. And Amazon . . . Well, Amazon measures everything because they sell everything! You get my point. If you ask Tesla how many cars they sold last month or Chick-fil-A how many sandwiches they sold last year, I guarantee they know.

The primary products of the church, according to Jesus, are disciples. Disciples are what we make. So what does it say about our priorities if few churches could tell you how many they made last year? Unfortunately, most churches have no measurements for discipleship. It's in our mission statement but not in our measurements.

> Most churches have no measurements for discipleship. It's in our mission statement but not in our measurements.

We measure what matters most.

As I've mentioned already, the reality is that most churches measure butts, budgets, and buildings. We count the attendance, we count the money, and we count the property. These are necessary things to count. I get that. If churches weren't responsible in these areas, then we wouldn't be good stewards with what God has given us. However, it does seem strange that we'd never consider *not* counting Sunday giving or Sunday attendance, but we have little issue with not counting the disciples we are making. I'll say it again. What we count and what we celebrate create our culture.

Butts, budgets, and buildings are all vital. It's like our pulse. If you don't have a pulse, you're dead. However, a pulse alone is not the full measure of health. There are many people who have a pulse but live on Waffle House, Coke, and Blue Bell ice cream.

Just because a person is alive doesn't mean they are functioning at their full potential. I mean, they're eating at Waffle House, for crying out loud! They clearly don't care what they put in their bodies. But healthy people consider far more than their pulse. Healthy people measure what they eat, how much they eat, and how much they work out. One of my Crossfit friends always says, "It doesn't matter how much you work out if you don't eat healthy." In the same way, it doesn't matter how many people show up if they're not making disciples. So why don't we try spending less time on church growth strategies and more time on building a discipleship culture?

Here is the bottom line. The church's mission is not to go and make small groups. It's not to go and make an impact. It's not even to go and make new churches. The church's mission is to go and make disciples.

I'm convinced that Jesus' model isn't outdated. It's just forgotten. Possibly even neglected.

But you know what's awesome about going and making disciples?

When you do it, you end up with all the rest.

Always.

Show me a church that is making disciples, and I'll show you a church that is forming new small groups. Show me a church that is making disciples, and I'll show you a church that is making an impact. Show me a church that is making disciples, and I'll show you a church that is planting new churches. Show me a church that is making disciples, and I'll show you a church that looks a lot like Jesus.

We can't put the cart before the horse. Discipleship isn't a distraction. It isn't a luxury. It isn't even an option. Discipleship is the main objective. Jesus' last words should be our first priority.

CHAPTER 6

The Four Arenas
for Discipleship

Now that we have discussed the importance of discipleship, let's break down the process to see how it can play out in real life.

Earlier, I acknowledged that no one these days has time to add more things to their calendar. I suggested instead that we include one another in our calendars. How can we do that?

Places Where We Can Include Disciples in Our Lives

It's been my experience that there are four arenas for discipleship, four areas of life where we can include another believer: personal life, family life, work life, and church life.

I. PERSONAL LIFE

Every one of us has a personal life that we tend to each day. It involves our passions and our hobbies, the things we do for fun or discipline or for sheer curiosity. Why not invite someone to do them with us? We all have our morning routines. Maybe it's drinking coffee and reading the Bible. Perhaps it's going for an early morning jog. It could be grocery shopping, getting your nails done, or even taking a yoga class. Maybe it's hunting or fishing. Whatever it is, we could invite a disciple to come along with us. Not every time. Not even most of the time. But sometimes. If we are going to do these things alone, why not allow someone younger to do them with us?

Or maybe it's a weekend hobby like playing golf. How painful could it be to invite a young person to join your regular Saturday foursome? Okay, I guess that could be pretty painful. But seriously, consider bringing a younger disciple into these moments of leisure. You don't have to have an agenda or a lesson to teach them; just including them will be enough.

Take a look at this list and see if there is an area where you could include someone.

■ Hobbies
■ Working out
■ Spending time with your friends
■ Morning routine
■ Grocery shopping
■ Preparing meals
■ Recharging and Sabbathing

2. FAMILY LIFE

More than half of millennials come from divorced or single-parent households. Because of this, our generation is dying to know what a healthy, loving family looks like. Show us. Invite us. Allow your family to become our family. After all, only 26 percent of millennials are married. That's a lot of people sitting at home alone eating ramen noodles. But 69 percent say we want to be married. Show us what it looks like. We're not looking for a perfect marriage; we're looking for a real one. A marriage where God uses both parties to make each other more like Jesus. And although they may stumble along the way, the Spirit always picks them back up.

Not having a Christian father, I have found that following men in this part of their lives has been one of the most impactful things for me.

Here's a list of areas where you might naturally include a young person.

- Family meals
- Kids' games
- Devotions
- Babysitting
- Neighborhood events
- Weekend activities
- Vacations

> We're not looking for a perfect marriage; we're looking for a real one.

3. WORK LIFE

Learning how to be like Jesus is the essence of discipleship. But don't limit your vision of what needs to be included in discipleship. Discipleship is not just about showing a young person how to spend time with Jesus in prayer and Bible study. It's also about showing them how you run a business or practice medicine according to Christian virtues. The workplace may be one of the best places for discipleship, especially if it's with a coworker, because your making them better is helpful to the company. Look for ways you might include someone in the following areas.

- Meetings
- Projects
- Conferences or seminars
- Business trips
- Strategic team lunches
- Banquets

As a communicator, I've followed many other communicators. I once followed an evangelist named Sujo John when he spoke at Universal Studios on the tenth anniversary of the September 11 attacks. Sujo has an incredible story of how he survived in the Twin Towers. Sujo was on the eighty-first floor of one tower. His pregnant wife worked in the other. By the grace of God, they both survived, and God has used their testimony mightily.

Following him that weekend as his assistant allowed me to do anything and everything to make his life easier while on the road. But it also let me watch how he prepared his heart before he preached to thousands. There was even one very late night when we checked into a hotel for just three hours of sleep before we caught our next flight. He said, "This is the part of ministry no one gets to see and no one wants to do." I took that to heart. I saw that ministry must be a calling, not just a career. Without following Sujo up close, I never would have known that. I may have just idolized the stage without considering the sacrifice.

4. CHURCH LIFE

My generation has done a poor job of caring for Christ's bride. We think it's okay to love Jesus but not the bride for whom he gave his life. We'd never expect this to work in our friendships. "Blake, I love you, man. But I just can't stand your wife."

I think it's crucial to involve young people in your responsibilities at the church, no matter how "big" or "small" they are. It shows the weight and value behind investing your time, talent, and treasure in your church.

> Many millennials think it's okay to love Christ but not the bride for whom he gave his life.

I had the incredible experience of getting to live, for a time, with my pastor, Jerry Wagner. During this time, Jerry graciously included me in the shaping of his church plant, Mercy Street. We'd sit around and strategize about mission, discipleship, preaching, and diversity—it was great. The thing about Jerry, however, is that he's a no nonsense kind of guy, which can sometimes be uncomfortable.

One day he said to me, "Grant, you love the church, right?"

"Of course I do," I said.

"Then why," he asked, "aren't you giving financially toward your church?"

Dang, I thought. *Jerry just went there.*

I mumbled my way through an excuse or two, feeling kind of like Peter must have when Jesus said, "Do you love me? Then feed my sheep."

I realized that no one had ever asked me whether I gave money to my church. And since I had never heard my young friends talking about tithing, it was easy to justify my neglect of giving because I gave back through serving. But Jerry's question forced me to grapple with the reality that since I wasn't giving now when I had only a little, I probably wouldn't give later when (hopefully) I had more.

Church is one of the easiest arenas to invite people into. It's also one of the most important. If we're freaking out about all the millennials leaving the church right now, how bad do you think it'll be when there's none left to disciple the Z generation? We have only a small window of time. We urgently need young people who love Christ and his bride. So let them join you as you serve the church.

So where can you include the younger generation in church? Here's a list.

- Greeting
- Ushering
- Youth ministry
- Children's ministry
- Bible studies
- Sports leagues
- Foreign mission trips
- Work projects
- Elder or committee meetings
- Small group
- Message prep

Ground Rules for Disciples

I have a confession to make. I am a cat person. I almost didn't share this because the world is hell-bent on hating cats. I once hated them too, but I travel way too much to have a dog. Dogs are needy. I needed a pet that wouldn't care if I was gone for a few days. So when my brother came home with Vincent, a kitten he got from the pound for twenty dollars (they were having a sale; who knew pounds had sales?), I let him stay. Vincent is seriously the most curious cat in all the world. There's a spot I know I can always find him, and that is my windowsill. Night and day, Vincent looks down at the courtyard from my second-story apartment window. He watches people down there. He watches the birds, the squirrels, the water fountain. As I'm writing this, you can probably guess what Vincent is doing.

So one day I have this bright idea. I'm going to take Vincent on a walk. I've never seen someone walk a cat, but that only made me want to try it even more. So I took him down to the courtyard he stares at constantly. I thought surely he would run wild with curiosity. He ran, all right—right back inside! After months of looking down at that courtyard, Vincent was scared and intimidated by all of it. Once it got real, he freaked out.

I've found that young people struggle a lot like Vincent. They desperately want to learn from someone ahead of them, but when they're with someone older, they don't know what to do. It's all so new for them. So here's a hint. Start with the basics, set some ground rules, and show them how they can help both of you make the best use of the time.

Before They Follow You

Give the potential disciple an assignment. This usually weeds out those who like the idea of growing from those who can't live without it. If they won't do the first assignment, they most likely won't do any others.

I've also found that how it begins is how it ends. So I want them to know from the start that this discipleship will require work. It's sort of like Jesus telling Peter to cast the nets on the other side of the boat. After he accomplished the assignment, Jesus discipled him.

Here are some examples of assignments I give, but feel free to come up with ones that fit you. I ask my disciples to make a five-year plan for their life. I want them to chart out some physical, emotional, spiritual, and economic goals they want to reach over the next five years. I know man makes his plans and God establishes his steps, but most young people haven't even considered a plan, so—shocker!—God hasn't established any steps. We make plans, and plans change. I know that. But seeing my disciples' goals helps me be an advocate for where the disciples want to go. It also gives clarity on what I should include them in. Without knowing their goals, I'll struggle to know how to develop them and hold them accountable.

> Discipleship hinges more on the hunger of the disciple than on the availability of the discipler.

Another assignment I may give is to have them write down three areas they see I can develop them in. These areas tend to revolve around a competency they want to learn or a character trait they want to grow in.

Last, when asked to disciple someone, I will suggest a few events they can join me in during the next two weeks. If they make it work, I know they're serious, but if they don't even try, it's probably not a good fit. I want to know they're willing to move things around to follow me, because discipleship hinges more on their hunger than on my availability.

THE BEST DISCIPLESHIP CURRICULUM

One final thought here on the nuts and bolts of discipleship. Every time I speak at a conference to pastors on the necessity of discipleship, I know that among the first questions will be, "What curriculum would you recommend we use for discipleship?"

It's a great question with a simple answer.

The Bible.

Can we just agree at this point that content and curriculum isn't our problem? This generation has more access to biblical content, commentary, books, and sermons than any generation in human history. It's so easy. You don't even have to read a book anymore. Someone will read it to you. And if they read too slow, you can speed them up! Anything we want to know about theology, church history, and discipleship is a swipe away. So why then are we so biblically illiterate?

The answer: We don't read the Bible anymore. Instead of doing Bible studies, we do studies on people's studies of the Bible.

> We don't read the Bible anymore. Instead of doing Bible studies, we do studies on people's studies of the Bible.

We read other people's commentary on the Bible instead of having our own real experience with the Word. We live vicariously through other people's encounters with God. It's kind of like watching a movie. We like their story, but we miss out on our own.

Now, let me be clear. I think there is a place for books, commentaries, and sermons. I mean, after all, I *am* writing a book here. But I don't think the primary curriculum for small groups or discipleship should be much more than the most sufficient book ever given to us, the Bible. The Bible is the best curriculum you can find for this generation. It's more than curriculum. It's our daily bread.

It's very rare that I ever dig into my Bible and walk away thinking, *Ehhh, pretty good.*

No! I almost always walk away thinking, *Man, I need to read this thing more.* What else can you say that about? What other book so reliably delivers God?

It is no coincidence that the driest seasons of my life happen to be when I'm not in God's Word. But when I thrive is when I treat the Bible like oxygen to my lungs. It's necessary, not just daily but for every moment of life. Charles Spurgeon said, "A Bible that is falling apart usually belongs to someone who isn't."

This kind of intimacy with the Word is crucial for disciplers to model and for young people to develop, since truth is more "relative" than ever. Right and wrong is constantly moving when our culture defines it. What once was unspeakable now is applaudable. The culture is really scaring my parents' and grandparents' generation, but I think there may be a silver lining. As Christians, fake news and shifting values shouldn't frighten us. The darker the world gets, the brighter God's truth shines. Have you ever noticed that jewelers always set their best diamonds on black velvet? When everything is dark, people look for light. They look for hope. So stop criticizing darkness and start turning on the light.

The psalmist says, "Those who look to [the LORD] are radiant; their faces are never covered with shame" (Ps. 34:5). We are the light of the world. Radiance is the byproduct of looking at God. What if Christians were radiant in comparison with the world because they were not ruled by the opinions of Fakebook, a political figure, or a commentator on the news?

I've found that the more you mature in your relationship with God, the less you read the Bible like a newspaper and the more you read it like a personal letter. One of the best things we can do for this generation is simply give them the letters God wrote to them.

We just have to remember that discipleship is a lot more of a map than a menu. It has a lot more to do with

> Stop criticizing darkness and start turning on the light.

taking a person *somewhere* than with teaching them *something*. Because if you think about it, what kind of class and curriculum did Jesus take his disciples through? It was the Bible, but it wasn't a classroom. It wasn't a lecture. It was a lab. He didn't say, "Come and learn." He said, "Come and follow me."

Jesus knew, as we do, that discipleship isn't just transferring information. It's transformative replication. Consider this as you view the graph on how students learn best. Look at this pyramid and ask yourself, "Where would I place Christ, and where would I place the church?"

The next chapter will focus on how we spend most of our time at the bottom of the pyramid.

THE **LEARNING** PYRAMID:

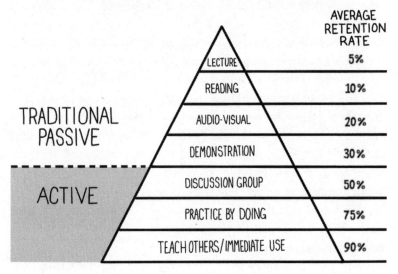

	AVERAGE RETENTION RATE
LECTURE	5%
READING	10%
AUDIO-VISUAL	20%
DEMONSTRATION	30%
DISCUSSION GROUP	50%
PRACTICE BY DOING	75%
TEACH OTHERS/IMMEDIATE USE	90%

TRADITIONAL PASSIVE

ACTIVE

The four arenas for Discipleship:

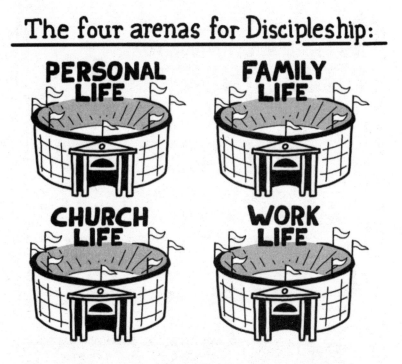

PERSONAL LIFE

FAMILY LIFE

CHURCH LIFE

WORK LIFE

DISCIPLESHIP HINGES on the HUNGER of the DISCIPLE MORE THAN THE AVAILABILITY of the one DISCIPLING

CHAPTER 7

THE POSTURES, PHASES, AND STAGES OF DISCIPLESHIP

The first guy I ever discipled was Nick. I was in college, and he was a freshman. He approached me to disciple him, and I was hesitant.

I was hesitant because I didn't feel ready. I thought I needed to be more spiritually mature. When I was discipled, it was by a married man with kids. But me, I was just a single guy with debt. What could I teach Nick?

Eventually, though, I came to the conclusion, *I may not be where I want to be, but I am not where I used to be, and I am spiritually a step ahead of him. So I'll offer him what I can.*

Another reason I was hesitant is because discipleship is so intrusive. I didn't want that type of accountability yet! If discipleship meant him joining my world, I didn't feel confident in every aspect of my life. I thought, *Yeah, I may be leading a nonprofit, but I also play a lot of* Call of Duty. *I'm not sure I want him to see how much I play video games with my free time. Yeah, I love to read, but I don't want him to see how much I don't study for school. Yeah, I'm disciplined for my age, except the inside of my car always looks like I'm moving.* I just didn't feel confident in his seeing the real me.

In the end, I let him in to see the good, the bad, and the ugly. He was better for it, and so was I, because it motivated me to get better. And it only gave me more respect for Jesus. How did this guy have twelve disciples around him for three years and never slip up?

Still, Nick himself made me hesitant too. He was a freshman in college and well, yeah, that says it all. He was gung ho about everything. He was outspoken. He always made sure the group and I knew what he thought. So there definitely were a few times when he'd join one of my meetings or come hang out with some of my friends, and I'd get that look that said, "Grant, who the heck is this guy?" It's kind of funny thinking about it now. But we were learning. I kept wondering, *How do I let him follow me as I follow Christ?*

He was so much like Peter—you know, a loose cannon type. But in my opinion, Peter gives hope to all passionate millennials. Peter always wanted to die on a hill for something. I mean, the dude cut a guy's ear off and thought he was being helpful! (Talk about a terrible evangelism strategy.) And then Jesus had to go fix Peter's mess. But Jesus just kept bringing him along. And now I think I get why. I'd rather have to channel someone's passion than motivate someone to *be* passionate. I'd rather tame a bull than train a donkey. I just needed some guidelines for Nick.

> I'd rather have to channel someone's passion than motivate someone to *be* passionate.

There needed to be rules.

There are certain settings where boundaries need to be made. I find this to be important when someone accompanies me in the workplace. I mean, you can't just have someone join you without a filter. There's a time for everything. In Ecclesiastes, it says there's a time to dance. There's a time to mourn. There's a time to sing, and there's a time to shut up. Or something like that.

I can't tell you how many people I've heard complain that when they have young people join them, they break all the rules. But it may not be out of arrogance. It could be out of ignorance. So when you start out on the path of discipling someone, you might want to teach them the three postures, the five phases, and the four stages of discipleship.

The Three Postures of Discipleship

1. *View.* The first job of a disciple is to simply watch and listen. They should be a fly on the wall. This was the first task of Jesus' disciples—to watch his every move. When does he pray? How does he pray? What does he most often study? In the beginning, a disciple's job is to take it all in, absorbing everything and asking questions at the appropriate time.

2. *Voice.* After a while, a disciple becomes familiar with you and your world. They've asked very good questions. They've taken very good notes. They are starting to catch on to how you think, how you answer questions, and how you handle situations. After that happens, you may reach a point where you feel comfortable with letting them share their perspective. I've found this to be common and especially beneficial in the workplace. It never hurts to have an outsider's perspective from a trusted young voice. I often tell young people, "Don't critique a problem unless you can create a solution." Pointing out problems is easy. Creating solutions is hard. If a young person works for you and follows you, they have an invested interest in contributing. Discipleship should be beneficial not just for him or her but also for the business.

3. *Vote.* When someone goes from being a fly on the wall as a "view" to contributing value as a "voice," you may have opportunities where you want them to be a "vote." A voter isn't just someone you think could add value; it's someone who *must* add value. Voters play a big role. Maybe even an equal role. This last posture of discipleship is a reward, a sign the disciple has submitted to the process, grown, and is now mature enough to make decisions on their own.

Voters may help decide what project to pursue, what person to hire, how to spend funds.

Don't be afraid to be transparent about all this, telling your disciple that you first expect them to quietly observe (view), before giving their opinion (voice), and that then, at the point you feel they have something to contribute, you may give them a position of power (vote). It clarifies the process, manages expectations, and gives young people a path to pursue.

THE FIVE PHASES OF DISCIPLESHIP

Another way to look at the process of discipleship is to break it down into five phases. You've probably heard of this before. It's the age-old plan for replication.

1. I do. You watch. We talk. This is like the view posture of discipleship. In this first stage, the disciple simply watches the person who is discipling him. Think about the disciples early on with Jesus. They needed to hear him preach and see him heal the sick before they could do anything on their own. Afterward they would ask him questions about what he was doing, and he would elaborate with them in private.

1. I DO. YOU WATCH. WE TALK.

2. I DO. YOU HELP. WE TALK.

3. YOU DO. I HELP. WE TALK.

4. YOU DO. I WATCH. WE TALK.

5. YOU DO. SOMEONE ELSE WATCHES.

2. *I do. You help. We talk.* The second phase begins to incorporate the disciple into the action of the discipler. The discipler is still the primary one doing the work, but the disciple is now beginning to assist (or, to use the posture analogy, beginning to find their voice). I like to think of this as the disciples passing out the loaves of bread to the five thousand. They weren't responsible for the miracle, but they were helping to administer the miracle.

3. *You do. I help. We talk.* The third phase involves the disciple beginning to act on his own. Think about the disciples being sent out to baptize and heal in the name of Jesus before they fully understood what they were doing. Sometimes they got it right, but then other times they would fail. Jesus coached them along as they went. It was trial and error, and this was totally okay. To use the posture analogy, the disciple is beginning to move from voice to vote.

> They weren't responsible for the miracle, but they were helping to administer the miracle.

4. *You do. I watch. We talk.* Eventually the disciples are left to carry on the work of Jesus after he ascends to the Father. So now the disciple is the one responsible for the action; they have full voting privileges. The disciple has learned what he needs from the discipler, and it's time to operate without an active chaperone, if you will. Of course, the disciple can always ring up the discipler for advice. Just like we can with Jesus through prayer. But now it's up to the disciple to do the work.

5. *You do. Somebody else watches. Y'all talk.* The final phase is for the disciple to become the discipler. The pattern now repeats itself. The student becomes the teacher by finding a new student. The disciples reproduced themselves by bringing new believers alongside them and teaching these new disciples to do what Jesus had taught them.

The cycle then goes on forever. Lather, rinse, repeat.

THE FOUR STAGES OF DISCIPLESHIP

So we've all encountered this at some point. We're just living our lives. Minding our own business. Living the dream. And then one day we get a Facebook message from someone we haven't seen in ages. What could it be? Why would they message me after all these years? Are they in trouble? Are they in need?

Nope. They're just trying to sell me some knives.

Oh, multilevel marketers. Whether you like them or not, you can't knock their hustle. They are motivated. One thing I appreciate about their work is, they have well-defined goals. They have stages. You may start out at the bronze level, but if you work hard, you hit silver, then gold, diamond, double diamond, and infinity stone!

I think it'd be helpful if the church had well-defined stages. It's hard to devote a lot of time to something if you don't know the point, the goals, or what a win looks like. In the following, I've tried to give some language that has worked for us. These are our four stages of discipleship.

1. Learner. Until you invite a person to follow you while you follow Christ, you are still in the learning phase. I don't care if you preach every Sunday, read Greek, and write bestselling books. If you have not invited someone to follow you in your walk with Christ, then you have yet to take the Great Commission seriously. To you, it's still just a good suggestion. In the words of John Maxwell, "If you think you're leading, but no one is following, then you're just taking a walk."

> "If you think you're leading, but no one is following, then you're just taking a walk."
>
> **—JOHN MAXWELL**

2. Leader. Leading means having at least one committed follower. Once you have explicitly invited someone to follow you, then you have moved from the learner stage to the leader stage. A lot of people think they're a leader simply because they influence or impact people. But that's how the world views leadership, not the church. The church has a higher standard, a focused plan. The church isn't called to just make an impact. The church is called to make disciples. Thus leading demands disciple making.

If you've become a leader, you're so close to being a disciple maker. You're on your way. Once your disciple starts discipling, then you've become a bona fide disciple maker. But you can't be a disciple maker until you make a disciple who disciples.

3. *Disciple maker.* This is where it gets fun, because you can see the real fruit. At this point, the people you once discipled are

DISCIPLESHIP DEVELOPMENT RAMP:

MULTIPLIER

DISCIPLE MAKER

LEADER

LEARNER

now out making other disciples, and it has nothing to do with you. You are, hopefully, off making even more disciples.

4. *Multiplier.* Multiplying is when your fruit has begun growing on other people's trees! Paul experienced this with Timothy when he said, "The things you have heard me say in the presence of many witnesses entrust to reliable people who will also be qualified to teach others" (2 Tim. 2:2). Paul, pouring into Timothy, asked Timothy to pour into others, who would in turn pour into others.

A Picture of True Disciple Making

Nothing fires me up more than seeing true disciple making in action. A few years ago, I was in Seattle, in the office of a pastor named Scott Dudley, when I noticed a framed picture that caught my attention. In the photo was Scott, an older man I didn't recognize, a young guy I did recognize, named Bryan, and then a high school kid.

"Scott," I asked, looking at the photo, "does this photo represent what I think it does?"

"What do you think it represents?"

"Well," I said, pointing at the older man in the photo, "I think this is the guy who discipled you. And I know you discipled Bryan. And I'm guessing that's the kid who Bryan disciples."

He grinned. "Yup. That's it!"

So check this out. The older man who discipled Scott had never met Bryan or his younger disciple. But because he had taken the time to disciple Scott, the effects were now rippling through two more generations. This picture was taken the first time they all met each other. It was a discipleship lineage, perhaps a discipleship legacy. It must have been pretty awesome for the older man to see the fruit of his labor.

I remember seeing that photo and thinking, *Man, one day I want to enter the gates of heaven not proud of all the sermons I've*

preached or books I've written but proud of all the disciples I've made.
I want to meet strangers in heaven who were discipled by my disciples.

Jesus spent three years discipling twelve guys, and his fruit is still growing! Roughly two billion people on earth call themselves Christians. Jesus set all this in motion in three years with twelve people. Think about what would happen if two billion Christians started discipling!

A multiplier is kingdom minded because he is constantly cultivating someone new. He isn't threatened by new young talent. He's thankful for it.

> Success without a successor is just temporary impact.

Because success without a successor is just temporary impact. And young passion without older wisdom is just a flash in the pan. Both need each other.

Today half of American pastors are older than fifty-five. In 1992, 24 percent were that old. Pastors sixty-five and older have almost tripled in the last twenty-five years, from 6 percent to 17 percent. Meanwhile, pastors forty and younger have fallen from 33 percent in 1992 to 15 percent today. So the older generation is holding on to leadership longer, while younger people are leaving the church sooner. I think there might be a correlation. The world is getting younger, while the church is getting older. Whether that's simply a result of increased longevity, fewer options for retired pastors, or, sadly, the older generation's desire to cling to power, the results are devastating, because many of these older leaders have no successor in place to take over when they leave.

> The older generation is holding on to leadership positions, while younger people are leaving the church.

Multipliers don't let this happen. They understand that if the church isn't investing in the future right now, it won't have much of a future at all.

The solution is discipleship. It may seem old school, but it's timeless. I think the Enemy sees our generational division and loves it. He wants to stifle the church. If you were the Enemy and you heard Jesus say, "The gates of hell cannot prevail against my church," you'd probably think, *Spoiler alert. I now know how it ends!* The Enemy knows he can't defeat the church. He can't

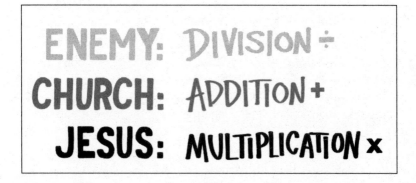

ENEMY: DIVISION ÷
CHURCH: ADDITION +
JESUS: MULTIPLICATION ×

even defend himself from the church. (Gates aren't an offensive weapon. Armies don't throw gates at each other.) But he's crafty. He can't defeat the church, so he attempts to divide the church. Just look around and you'll see it: race, denomination, education, and generation. I'm convinced division is the number one tool and strategy of the Enemy. He used it between Adam and Eve in the beginning, and he's using it in the church right now. So if that's his strategy, we have to elevate our strategy. He's trying to divide. We're trying to add. But Jesus wants to multiply.

FINAL REMINDER: DON'T DISCIPLE IN YOUR OWN STRENGTH

We can talk about the postures and phases of discipleship all we want, but in truth, discipleship will never get anywhere without *power*—the power of the Holy Spirit working in and through us, and of that same Holy Spirit working in and through our disciples.

This truth was conveyed to me in a powerful way when I started Initiative Network. I was privileged to join this massive gathering of Christian leaders from all over the world. We convened in the Big Apple. There was a lot of energy, and God was moving. The goal of the gathering was to share best practices. How is God working in major cities across the world? And what can we learn from each other? They had different rooms for different topics. The problem was, I was torn between two topics: prayer revivals and church planting.

The largest room definitely caught my attention. This was where church planting would be discussed. If you don't know, planting a church is basically every millennial pastor's dream. "Forget working for a church. I'm gonna start my own!" (Funny side note: Has anyone noticed that God always calls millennials to plant churches in cool cities? New York, San Francisco, Portland, LA, Seattle. God is so hipster! He never calls young people to stay where they are or to move to obscure, unheard-of places that don't have chic coffee shops. Or maybe we mute him when he does?)

Well, I was a typical young guy, starting a new thing, so I really wanted to go to the church-planting breakout. As you can expect, the room was packed with passion and plaid. It was the beardiest room I've ever been in—hundreds of millennials. And honestly, the content was incredible. Terrific insight on the necessary tactics to start a new church in a new city.

But after a while, the other topic started calling my name. I'm not a prayer warrior by any stretch of the imagination, but I've come to the end of my rope so many times, I've been given ample opportunity to see how powerful prayer is. So midway in, I snuck into the room on prayer, only to find out it was waaaaaay different than my last room. *Sesame Street* used to have a great song and skit with the lyrics, "One of these things is not like the other. One of these things just doesn't belong." I kind of felt that way when I walked in.

There weren't any millennials in the room. There weren't even any Xers. I left the church-planting room with hundreds of millennials for a prayer room with a handful of boomers.

They. Were. Awesome! They didn't really talk about prayer tactics. Instead they just prayed. They would share how God was starting a prayer revival in a city, and then they'd stop what they were doing and pray over it. There was a different type of passion in their room. It was boldness.

> When you're younger, you think you can change the world. But as you get older, you realize you can't change the world without the power of God.

At the end, I went up to Dimas Salaberrios, the man facilitating the group, to ask him the one question that had been burning a hole in my brain. I said, "Why do you think there's so many passionate young leaders in the church-planting breakout, and there's only a few among the older generation in this breakout?"

Like a Christian Yoda, he said, "When you're younger, you think you can change the world. But as you get older, you realize you can't change the world without the power of God."

He was right. It's easy to find passionate millennials. It's hard to find prayerful ones. That truth really rocked me for the next couple of days. I went home thinking, *What if my generation, with all their passion and childlike faith, could pursue changing the world first in prayer?*

There's a saying we have at Initiative: "Prayer is the work. Ministry is the reward." A wise friend named Tomi told us this when we first started our ministry, and I think it's a great reminder to all of us.

Don't disciple out of your own strength. It's exhausting and it's impossible.

Not Alone

I've talked a lot about the Great Commission and the importance of making disciples. But I also want to remind you of the missing message in the Great Commission, one that is crucial for us to remember. We forget that the last words of Christ to his disciples are, "Surely I am with you always, to the very end of the age" (Matt. 28:20).

> We can have small faith, but it must be in a big God. Even faith the size of a mustard seed will do.

Hear that? Christ is with us. We're not alone.

We, as believers, have an advantage. We don't have to have the biggest faith. We can have small faith, but it must be in a big God.

Even faith the size of a mustard seed will do. Because on the other end of our faith is a mountain-moving, sea-parting, heart-changing, grace-giving kind of God. Don't feel like you're doing discipleship alone. Don't even try to *be* better. Just *believe* better.

Before Jesus commissions us, he says, "All authority in heaven and on earth has been given to me" (v. 18).

After he commissions us, he says, "And surely I am with you always, to the very end of the age" (v. 20).

He's not asking you to do any of this alone. He's already gone before you. Like a gentleman who's arranged a well-orchestrated date, he's just asking for you to join him and enjoy the ride.

CHAPTER 8

COMMON EXCUSES FOR NEGLECTING DISCIPLESHIP

I don't believe most Christians choose to neglect discipleship. I think it's simply not on their radar. It's like not investing in my 401k. With each passing month, I don't say, "Shoot! I missed another month of investing in my retirement." Nope. I don't even think about it because it's so far off my radar.

The same thing goes for Christians and discipleship. It's so normal not to do it that we don't feel bad when we don't. We are perfectly comfortable in a brand of Christianity that calls people to attend church but not follow Jesus' way.

But if you read the New Testament, you can't find any support for this version of Christianity. In fact, Dietrich Bonhoeffer once said, "Christianity without discipleship is Christianity without Christ." Essentially, we have to ignore major parts of Christ's life in order to ignore the importance of discipleship.

So what is our excuse? Why do only 17 percent of Christians say they meet with a spiritual mentor as part of their discipleship efforts? Why does discipleship seem so far-fetched to expect from the everyday Christian? Well, let's get into it. These are the most common excuses I've heard for why Christians don't disciple anyone.

"I DON'T HAVE TIME"

You're right. You don't. Who does? Nobody has time for disciple-ship! You're too busy. We're *all* too busy. Can you remember the last time you asked somebody how they were doing, and they *didn't* tell you they were busy? It's an epidemic, but that's a topic for an entirely different book.

The beautiful thing about shifting from mentoring to disci-pleship is that you don't have to create more time, because you don't have to add anyone to your calendar. You just need to *include* someone in it.

This requires younger Christians to be willing to adjust their schedule for the older Christian who is willing to disciple them. The young person needs to change their life to fit into yours, just like the disciples did for Jesus. Jesus basically made the disciples go on a three-year camping trip. And they went for it. The young person looking to be discipled needs to display this kind of willing-ness to adapt their life.

I'll be honest. I'm not always willing to do this. But recently I was. I met an older, successful, and more mature Christian I wanted to be discipled by. The problem was, he was a very, very busy man. He owns the architect firm for this small start-up out of Arkansas called Walmart. Apparently the start-up is doing pretty well, so Raymond is always on the go. I knew if I asked him to disciple me, he'd say he was too busy. But I also knew he was a very disciplined runner, and at the time I was trying to get into running. So one day, while we were in NYC for the same event, I asked him if we could run together in Central Park. Unfortunately, it just didn't work out. So when we got back to Dallas, I texted him, asking if I could run with him, and he said, "Yes. Let's do it. I'm actually going tomorrow."

"Great. What time should I meet you?" I asked.

"Four. Meet me at my office, and we'll run from there."

Four a.m.?! Oh wow. My mind was telling me no, but my body—my body was telling me no as well. But still, I decided I would do it, even though I thought he was crazy to go running at four in the morning. He was one of those enthusiastic half marathon runners, and if that's what it was going to take to get time with him, I'd move my schedule to make it work. I looked at my calendar and, surprisingly, I didn't have anything booked at 4:00 a.m.

The next morning I woke up earlier than I have in years to go meet him at his office downtown for our crazy pre-dawn exercise. I'd love to tell you it was my best discipleship experience, but it wasn't. Quite the opposite. He wasn't there. I waited. And waited. And waited. He never came. He woke up hours later to my text messages and replied, "I'm so sorry, Grant! You thought I meant four in the morning? I meant four in the afternoon!"

I'm thinking, "Well, yeah! Who the heck runs at 4:00 p.m.?" I was kind of glad, though, that he didn't show. He now knew I was willing to run at any hour to get time with him. I don't tell this story to toot my horn, because, believe me, I don't always get this right. But we millennials have to be willing to adapt our schedule to fit into the schedules of others. It can't be the other way around. We can't ask the older generations to come to us. We must go to them.

If we do this, they will know we are serious, and they'll be more likely to dedicate time to us. Showing up at four in the morning might have made me look silly, but you know what it also did? It made me look committed. It made me look *hungry*.

Great leaders want to develop other leaders. They're not looking for projects. They're looking for protégés—emerging leaders they can maximize. But great leaders can't afford to waste valuable time and energy on just anyone. What they want is a person who is committed to the journey, actively working toward whatever goal or career it is they are pursuing. They don't want to start the fire; they want to pour gasoline on one. It's similar to *Shark Tank*. They're

> Great leaders don't want to start the fire; they want to pour gasoline on one.

not looking for new businesses. They're looking for *successful* new businesses. That's who gets their investment.

Henry Blackaby put it like this: "Go where God is already moving." So look for someone whose heart is on fire. God is already on the move in their life. Now invite them into your life and fan that flame by discipling them.

"I Don't Feel Qualified or Equipped"

Once again, you're right. You're not qualified or equipped. Nobody is. Were the disciples qualified? Nope. They were the opposite of qualified, having already washed out of the rabbi-in-training system. Their culture had deemed them unworthy of studying under a rabbi, but Jesus invited them anyway. You don't need to be qualified, only willing. God equips as God calls. We just have to go and be willing to trust that he will give us what we need to get the job done.

You must remember that young people want you to be real, more than they want you to be right. I've found many mothers who don't want to invite young girls into their homes because their house is a mess. But do you know the difference between the homes of confident, disciple-making moms and those of moms who are embarrassed to invite young people in?

> Young people want you to be real, more than they want you to be right.

Nothing. Both houses are usually a mess!

Young Christian women do not flock to the homes of people who have really clean houses. They flock to the homes that are open.

I met a great mom who always said to young girls who wanted to be discipled by her, "Look. You can come into my world and see into my life, but don't expect a perfect life or a perfect home. You're going to see what real life looks like when you're trying to raise three kids. The house is going to be a mess sometimes, and there's a good chance I'll even ask you to help out while you're around. Are you okay with that?"

Absolutely! This mom just gave girls who have been sold a lie from Hollywood and Instagram for years a taste of reality and a path to grow as a wife and mother.

Discipleship isn't about inviting someone to witness your perfect life. It's about inviting someone to join your imperfect life that's being transformed by a perfect Christ. If we all waited until we were without sin to disciple someone, nobody would ever get discipled.

Discipleship requires that people see your junk. I'm sorry, it just does.

I understand this is difficult for older generations, who were taught to keep their struggles private. But consider John Maxwell's advice: "If you want to impress people share your successes. If you want to impact people share your failures."

> If we all waited until we were without sin to disciple someone, nobody would ever get discipled.

Don't forget, Jesus didn't just allow his disciples to see him make the lame walk and the blind see, he also let them see him weep in the garden of Gethsemane.

One path says, "I'm equipped. Follow me." The other path says, "I'm not equipped, but I'm one step ahead. Follow me as I follow Christ." Which one sounds like God's path for us?

"I Don't Know Enough about the Bible"

Great. Neither did the disciples! They were not biblical scholars by any stretch of the imagination. You don't have to be one either.

You may not be a great orator, but you may be a pretty good father or mother. You may not be a great end-times theologian, but you may be a pretty good husband or wife. You may not be a great evangelist, like Billy Graham, but you may be a pretty good neighbor. Remember the apostle Paul's words to the Thessalonians: "Because we loved you so much, we were delighted to share with you not only the gospel of God but our lives as well" (1 Thess. 2:8). I can't tell you how many young adults have heard the gospel for years but haven't seen it in months. Just be who God created you to be, and he will take care of the rest.

Tony Evans is easily one of the best Bible teachers of our time. This is a man who could never say, "I don't know my Bible well." His kids are all crushing it at walking with the Lord and living into their calling. Anthony Evans is an extremely gifted musician. Jonathan Evans is the chaplain for the Cowboys. Priscilla Shirer is a renowned speaker and talented actress. Chrystal Evans Hurst is a new author and prominent women's ministry leader. Tony Evans must be one proud dad!

So when I got to meet him one day, I had to ask him a question about parenting: "What single thing do you think attributed the most to the spiritual maturity of your kids today?"

His answer? The table.

He shared how intentional they were at the table while the kids were growing up. They would pray. They would share about their lives. They'd highlight a missionary family, and the kids would give of their allowance. They would discuss any tensions among the family. They'd introduce new friends or potential dates at the table. Everything happened at the table. And to this day, at least once a month they still all get together around the table.

I share this because Tony could have accredited his kids' spiritual maturity to so many things. The pulpit. The Bible. The church. But he said, "The table." And in a way, he leveraged the table like a pulpit. His influence was Psalm 128:3–4: "Your wife will be like a fruitful vine within your house; your children will be like olive shoots around your table. Yes, this will be the blessing for the man who fears the Lord."

I want to encourage you to start with the table. You don't need to be some great Bible expositor like Tony Evans to raise spiritually mature children. Simply start with a meal and see where God takes your family.

"I'M NOT DISCIPLING ANYONE RIGHT NOW, BUT I AM . . ."

It's often said that millennials are one of the most biblically illiterate generations our nation has ever seen. I think this is true. But I think there's a bigger problem.

Let's try an experiment. What percent of the Bible would you say you've read? Ten percent? Twenty-five percent? Fifty percent? Seventy-five percent? One hundred percent?

Write down the percent you'd guess. _____

So if that's how much you know, what percent of that do you actually obey?

Have you been *praying for your enemies* this month?

Have you been *Sabbathing* this month?

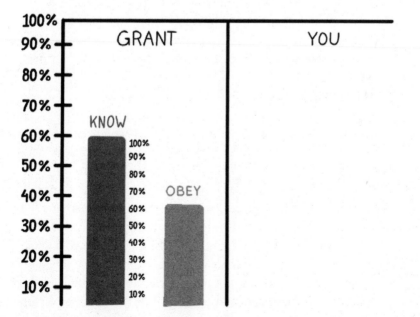

Have you *loved the Lord your God with all your heart, soul, and mind* this month?

Write down the percent you'd guess. _____

I've never asked someone this question and heard them confidently say they obey even 70 percent of what they know. For me, I'd say I know maybe 60 percent of the Bible. But on a good day, I probably obey only 60 percent of the 60 percent I know.

> Our problem is not how biblically illiterate we are but how biblically *disobedient* we are.

My point in showing this visual is to highlight our real problem. One hundred percent of Christians know more Bible than they obey.

Yes, Christians are biblically illiterate. Especially millennials. But our problem isn't how biblically illiterate we are. It's how biblically *disobedient* we are.

I think we're at the point where people need to see the Word, not just hear it. The Word displayed through obedience is quite compelling. Discipleship requires you to teach someone to *observe and obey* all that God has commanded us. Not just hear and memorize.

Samuel said to King Saul, "To obey is better than sacrifice" (1 Sam. 15:22).

With discipleship, I've found that many think, *Well, I'm not discipling anyone, but I am . . .*

There is no good answer at the end of that sentence.

There is no sacrifice great enough to negate our lack of obedience. And choosing not to obey is choosing to disobey. It's the same when someone calls you. You can swipe it green to answer, you can swipe it red to decline, or you can ignore it altogether. One response answers the call; the other responses decline the call.

I hope this discipleship message is like a pebble in your shoe. You just can't ignore it. It bothers you every time you try to go on with your walk. This calling got me one day, and it was one of the best things that ever happened to me. I didn't know discipleship was a missing part of my life. But once I did, it bothered me until I started pursuing it.

The first step on any road to recovery is admitting there is a problem. If we can't admit that we are being disobedient in our refusal to disciple, I don't think we are going to be ready to make the big changes necessary for discipleship.

"I CAN'T FIND ANYONE TO DISCIPLE"

"Well," you say, "I'd like to disciple someone, but I don't know who I should disciple!" This is a warranted concern. Our generations are divided, so it's hard for both parties to connect.

The first response is prayer. Pray that God would make it clear who you should pour into, whether it's someone you already know or someone he'll introduce you to. God has a knack for connecting his children. He's a master chessman, especially for those who make themselves available. He connected Samuel to David, Naomi to Ruth, Peter to Cornelius, Philip to the Ethiopian eunuch, and Simon the tanner to Paul. I don't think God is done introducing his people for his purposes. So pray, expect, and respond.

Acts 17:26 says, "From one man he made every nation of men, that they should inhabit the whole earth; and he determined the times set for them and the exact places where they should live" (NIV 1984). God has us in our city, in our job, at this time, for his purposes. This verse is mostly used for evangelism, but I think the principle is also true for discipleship. I believe many of us are already in relation with the right candidates to disciple. I'd say the best place to start is your work, and then your church. Here's why I say work first.

- *Relevant.* Twenty-eight percent of millennials have a side hustle to supplement their main income.[13] This is such an opportunity! If this generation has such a propensity toward entrepreneurial endeavors, why not connect them to successful Christian business leaders? This generation wants to get farther *faster*. The marketplace is a great environment to learn the good, the bad, and the beautiful of faithfully working unto the Lord.

- *Proximity.* When you disciple someone you work with, you'll naturally cross paths all the time. Some of my best disciples have worked for me or with me. You just can't beat time together.
- *Delegation.* It benefits the company for you to develop someone younger. They become a greater asset. You're also able to delegate responsibilities in the workplace. In turn, they're able to lighten your load. Plus, it increases the retention rate of young people because for them it's no longer just a job or a faceless institution. Now it's a training ground. Now it's a personal friendship.
- *Opportunity.* In your workplace, there's more opportunity to professionally disciple someone outside the faith. There's a lot of debate as to whether the disciples became Christians as soon as they started following Jesus or somewhere along the process. I kind of think it was along the way. What if you could do the same for somebody in your workplace?

If there's no one at work, then search the church. And I do mean *the* church, not necessarily *your* church. Of course, the ideal place to find someone would be in your own church, because then you'll naturally cross paths, but many times congregations are either younger or older. So both parties often ask me where to find each other. There are pretty limited options, and I'd encourage you not to limit yourself to only your church. Except for Kevin when I was sixteen, I've never been discipled by someone who goes to my church.

Last but not least, just try to become a regular where young people are. I always tell young people, if you're not often the youngest person in the room, you're in the wrong rooms. But vice versa, we need some seasoned leaders who would tithe their time to younger groups. If you want to find a young disciple, diversify your routine. One of my board members, Paige, just shows up. All the time. She shows up at our small monthly prayer nights. She shows up at our big worship nights. She shows up at the parties we throw. She just shows up, and she's got the younger girls to prove it. All the girls want some time with Paige. She's a regular. Question: Are you a regular in any groups that don't look like you?

> Are you a regular in any groups that don't look like you? Jesus was.

Jesus was.

I promise you, if you want to see God move in mighty ways, switch up your playground and your playmates.

CHAPTER 9

Five Qualities to Look For in a Disciple

I went to a Bible study a few years back. It was for the "silver saints" in the church. Their words, not mine. After my speech on the importance of discipleship even after retirement, a woman came up to me and said with tears in her eyes, "Grant, I love what you're saying, but do you honestly think any young person would actually want to be discipled by a woman like me?" It nearly broke my heart because I could see that she wanted to disciple someone but didn't believe anybody had the interest.

I apologized to her. I realized in that moment how bad a job my generation has done to honor the generations before ours. With all the rapid changes over the last few decades, we've lost our appreciation for those who gave a lot of blood, sweat, and tears for the opportunities we get to enjoy today. What's worse, I've found that many in older generations don't feel like the younger generation even wants to learn from them. We've come off like we've got it all together and they're old-fashioned. We've discovered the new way, and they're just in the way. This is a fear among the church's elders. With all this focus on the millennials and the next generation, what will happen to those who built the church? Will they just be displaced and forgotten?

It's never worked out when young people surround themselves

only with each other. It's like freshmen asking other freshmen for dating advice. I'm thinking, *Bro, the last girl you dated was from Tinder! Why would I ask you for advice? I need to talk to someone in a healthy marriage.* Let's be real. Youth is never associated with wisdom in the Bible, but gray hair is.

However, I'm not going to lie. Unfortunately, not every young person is looking for someone older and wiser. They haven't learned the benefits of honor and hunger. I wish I could say every millennial is ready to be discipled, but they're not. Moreover, I believe discipleship hinges on the hunger of the disciple.

I offer my disciples access to my online calendar, so they have free rein to join whatever sparks their interest. But I've noticed that the hungry ones join the most and grow the most, and the others eventually don't work out. So I put together a list of five qualities that are all great signs of a ready disciple. I may not find someone with all of these characteristics, but when they have most of them, I get excited for what God has in store for us.

THE FIVE QUALITIES TO LOOK FOR IN A DISCIPLE

1. A DISCIPLE MUST BE FAITHFUL

Discipleship simply does not work if the disciple cannot follow through and do what he says he is going to do. A yes must mean yes, and a no must mean no. If a disciple cannot keep their word, then the discipler cannot do their job.

God never breaks his word. If God did, we wouldn't trust him. But God is faithful; he always follows through. Keeping our word and being faithful to our commitments is one of the primary ways we honor the One in whose image we have been made.

Being faithful can cover a multitude of sins. Think about the disciples. They messed up all, the, time. They didn't know much or have great character, but they had huge commitment. Along the way, they cut off a man's ear, they fell asleep during prayer, and they jockeyed for positions of honor. Once they were rebuked by Jesus because they asked if they could call fire down from heaven to destroy some Samaritans. And we can't forget that time Jesus called Peter "Satan." That's never a good sign. But despite their shortcomings, they stayed faithful. In the end, they went to their graves totally committed to Jesus.

- *Peter*: crucified upside down
- *Andrew*: scourged and then crucified in AD 69
- *James (Son of Zebedee)*: killed with a sword
- *John*: exiled
- *Philip*: scourged, thrown into prison, and crucified in AD 54
- *Bartholomew*: skinned alive and then beheaded
- *Thomas*: speared to death
- *Matthew*: stabbed in the back
- *James (Son of Alphaeus)*: stoned and then hit in the head with a club
- *Thaddaeus*: crucified in AD 72
- *Simon*: crucified in AD 74

I think there's a huge misconception about investing in someone younger only if they have character and if they are competent. But I think Jesus was more interested in commitment than in character. Because if you have character and your disciple is committed, then eventually your character will rub off on them. It's what happened with the disciples. These men may not have been our first choice, but no one can argue they weren't faithful to Jesus Christ—both the man and his message.

2. A DISCIPLE MUST BE AVAILABLE

A disciple must adapt to the schedule of the discipler. A young person can have the best intentions in the world, but if they aren't flexible with their time, it'll just never happen. A disciple must be willing to join the discipler on his journey. Discipleship cannot happen remotely. The onus is on the disciple to change their location or schedule to accommodate the discipler.

Consider what James and John were willing to do when Jesus called them. "He saw two other brothers, James son of Zebedee and his brother John. They were in a boat with their father Zebedee, preparing their nets. Jesus called them, and immediately they left the boat and their father and followed him" (Matt. 4:21–22).

I love the imagery here. The Bible says they immediately left their boat. I like to imagine James and John jumping out of the boat and swimming to shore because they were just that serious. Their dad goes home with the fish. He walks in the front door and says, "Honey, I'm home."

The mom, who is in the living room reading *The Purpose Driven Wife*, asks, "Where are the boys?"

"Oh," Zebedee says, "something happened. They went to be with the Lord."

"What!"

"No, I mean, they *literally* went to be with the Lord."

I'm pretty sure that's exactly how it went down.

What I love about this story is that James and John left everything they knew to follow Jesus.

> The disciples left behind everything. A disciple must be willing to at least leave behind *something*.

Of course, your disciple doesn't need to be that serious, but if they can't or won't move their life around in order to be in close proximity with you, then discipleship will not be possible. Mentorship yes, but not discipleship.

The disciples left behind everything. A disciple must be willing to at least leave behind *something*.

3. A DISCIPLE MUST BE TEACHABLE

Jesus required his disciples to be teachable. No matter what. It didn't matter what other incredible gifts you might bring to the table. If you weren't teachable, you weren't a disciple. A disciple's posture was more important than their potential.

Consider the tale of the rich young ruler versus the tale of Peter.

Jesus and his disciples were poor. They were always sleeping in different places and wondering where the next meal was coming from. So you'd think that when the rich young ruler showed up, Jesus would have jumped at the chance to have this guy tag along. He had money, influence, and power. With his resources, he could have easily maximized the message. But Jesus had the same requirements for him as for the others. Sell all your stuff, Jesus said, and follow me. But the rich young ruler just couldn't do it. He missed out on becoming the thirteenth disciple because he chose the treasures of life over the teachings

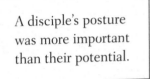

A disciple's posture was more important than their potential.

of Christ! I find that so crazy to think about. But this is even more crazy: Jesus just lets him go. If the guy isn't teachable, Jesus doesn't need his money.

Now contrast that story with Peter's. Peter was just a nothing fisherman with a reputation for being a hothead. Or in the words of my pastor, Jerry Wagner, "Peter must have had peppermint socks, because he was always getting his foot stuck in his mouth." On paper, he had a lot less to offer Jesus than did the rich young ruler.

But here is how Peter's calling went down. Jesus sees him one morning standing on the shore with some other fishermen, washing the nets. Peter had a bad night, not catching anything. Jesus tells him to take his boat back out and try once more. Peter had no reason to trust Jesus and every reason to question him. Who was this guy, anyway? Peter was a fisherman, and this was some random carpenter's son. What good would it do to throw out the nets again?

But Peter listened and did what Jesus said, and he caught enough fish to start his own Long John Silver's. The rest is history.

Trust is at the core of having a teachable spirit. Both Peter and the rich young ruler had to trust that Jesus knew better, even though it didn't make sense. Moreover, Jesus didn't just ask them to trust him with something small. He asked them to trust him with something they were *identified for*. As a poor man, he told a rich man what to do with his money, and as a carpenter, he told a fisherman what to do with his nets.

One man had a teachable spirit and went on to preach to thousands. The other trusted what he knew and remained nameless, a footnote and a lesson in poor choices.

4. A DISCIPLE MUST BE COMPATIBLE

Okay, this one might sound a little weird to you, but bear with me. The initial stages of discipleship are just like dating.

Chemistry matters. The discipler and the disciple don't necessarily have to have a lot in common, but there does need to be some kind of spark between them. If there is, just as in dating, the relationship will be far more dynamic.

It's also similar to dating in the sense that the disciple needs to confidently ask the discipler for his or her discipleship. Nobody wants to be asked out by a person with no confidence. Disciples need to be confident with their intentions and let the discipler know they really want to do this.

Moreover, it's good to get to know someone before dating them. Same thing with discipleship. Have a few meetings and take your time getting to know one another, so you can decide whether there is some chemistry, whether you'll be compatible. Sometimes you'll know within five minutes. Other times you'll need longer. Just like dating.

Finally, everyone gets rejected in dating. It happens in discipleship too. When it does, the disciple can't give up. It hurts when someone says no, but if a person really wants to be discipled, they will continue pursuing a discipler until they find the right one, someone with whom they are compatible. A disciple can never give up hope.

5. A DISCIPLE MUST BE HUNGRY

Over the years, I've had young people reach out to me for disciple-ship. And this is what I have found. They have good intentions, but often they are just not hungry enough. How do I know?

They don't ask questions.

Do you realize that most of the teachings we have from Christ aren't from his flashy new sermon series? They're from people constantly asking him questions, especially his disciples!

Jesus was asked more than 183 questions in the Gospels.

> Most of the teachings we have from Christ aren't from his flashy new sermon series. They're from his disciples constantly asking him questions.

Jesus himself asked more than three hundred questions!

Questions are central to discipleship. The disciples constantly asked Jesus questions because they were constantly seeking clarity. They were desperately hungry for it.

Think about this. Most of us have the Lord's Prayer memorized, right? We do because the disciples asked a simple question.

Recall the story: "One day Jesus was praying in a certain place. When he finished, one of his disciples said to him, 'Lord, teach us to pray, just as John taught his disciples.' He said to them, 'When you pray, say: "Father, hallowed be your name . . .'"'" (Luke 11:1–2).

The rest is history.

If your disciple isn't hungry, it's going to be hard to feed them. My best disciples have had an insatiable desire to learn. I'm not *just* trying to have someone follow me. I'm trying to make them a fisher of men. That's impossible if they just want to ambiguously follow me and have me guide the whole discussion. They've got to be hungry. They've got to ask questions.

To sum it all up, potential disciples should be faithful, available, teachable, compatible, and hungry.

CHAPTER 10

DISCIPLESHIP REFORMATION

When you study the history of the church, you see that every five hundred years something incredible happens. The church experiences a reformation. It reforms itself into something new. The result of these reformations is that the gospel is carried forward into the world in novel ways.

The first reformation took place around the year 500, in what was called the monastic movement. During this period, Christian monks carried the gospel all over Europe, establishing monasteries where the faithful could keep the faith alive through sacred prayer, study, and worship. These monasteries became the foundation for the evangelization of Europe.

Five hundred years later, in 1054, the church experienced what came to be known as the Great Schism. Until this point, the church had been one unified whole, but it was now split into two factions: the East and the West. The church in the West became known as the Roman Catholic Church, and the church in the East became known as the Eastern Orthodox Church. The schism was the result of many factors, some cultural, some theological, and some down-right ridiculous. The result, however, was that each church, both in the East and in the West, developed rich canonical heritages that helped spread the faith powerfully throughout the world.

Five hundred years later, it happened again with the Protestant Reformation. You probably are most familiar with this reformation.

In 1517, Martin Luther published his ninety-five theses protesting some of the practices and beliefs of the Catholic Church, and a new era in church history was born. A lot changed during this time, but basically there was a transfer of power from the clergy to the people. And with the advent of the printing press, the Bible was suddenly thrust into the people's hands, and they were empowered to read it on their own, apart from the heavy-handed authority of the church.

I don't think it's a coincidence that I'm finishing this book during the month of the five hundredth anniversary of the Protestant Reformation, as we are experiencing another monumental shift in power. I think the church is ready for a reformation. Below are just some key similarities between the state of the church back then and the state of the church now.

The Word of God Then; the Work of God Now

As we all know, Luther's ninety-five theses changed everything. It was one of the most significant events not just in church history but in all of human history.

That said, my favorite thing about the Reformation is actually what Luther did after his ninety-five theses. He did something that today is taken for granted but back then was downright scandalous.

Martin Luther gave power to the people. He gave them the Word of God.

Reformations happen when you give people power. It's disruptive.

As mentioned before, Uber disrupted the car industry when it gave people power. Airbnb disrupted the hotel industry when it gave people power. Martin Luther disrupted the church when it gave people power. And we could disrupt the world if we gave people power. Discipleship is a platform that multiplies, disrupts, and maybe even reforms.

The Printing Press to a Facebook Post

There's never been a time like today when you can succeed without the institution supporting you. You can be a successful musician without a label, a successful author without a publisher, a successful entrepreneur without a storefront, and even a successful presidential nominee without a party. Platforms like YouTube, Twitter, Instagram, Spotify, Soundcloud, and Etsy have opened the door for the everyday visionary.

Any person with a phone can become a worldwide evangelist within minutes. Consider Jeff Bethke. He created a simple online video of himself performing a spoken word poem about why he loves Jesus but hates religion, and the thing went viral. Before he knew it, he gained an audience of millions and was able to speak truth powerfully in outlets such as CNN and Fox News. Now he and his wife have an international ministry online that reaches millions. All because of one YouTube video.

I believe social media is the modern day printing press. It gives a voice to the voiceless.

American statistician Nate Silver said, "The Protestant Reformation had a lot to do with the printing press, where Martin Luther's theses were reproduced about 250,000 times, and so you had widespread dissemination of ideas that hadn't circulated in the mainstream before."

We find ourselves in a day when anyone's voice can go viral, as long as they have something revolutionary to say.

Theology Divides, Mission Unites

Because the last reformation gave us the Word, it also gave us theology. Unfortunately, theology tends to divide us. For example, there are now thirty-three thousand Christian denominations in the world. (Baskin Robbins has nothing on us! We've got all the flavors.) Although that wasn't the goal of the Reformation, it was more than just one split. It spread into thousands of splits. But luckily, mission has always brought us together. Just watch a crisis occur and you'll see God's people respond. Whether it's responding to 9/11 or Hurricane Harvey, God's people come together to serve those in need, and we couldn't care less about our denominational differences in those moments. It's simply what Jesus would do. Love, serve, and engage. While theology may divide us, Christ mission unites us.

FROM CLERGY-CONTROLLED TO PASTOR-DEPENDENT

Martin Luther translated the Word of God into German because the Catholic clergy controlled the interpretation. At the time, the Catholic Church was selling indulgences so you (or a loved one) could speed your way through purgatory and get to heaven as quickly as possible. There was also a heavy emphasis on works. Luther believed that the Catholic clergy were often misleading the people of God with false interpretations of the Scriptures. He said, "A simple layman armed with Scripture is to be believed above a pope or a council without it." And Luther disagreed with the loose authentication and elevation of relics. He said, "What lies there are about relics! One claims to have a feather from the wing of the angel Gabriel, and the Bishop of Mainz has a flame from Moses' burning bush. And how does it happen that eighteen apostles are buried in Germany when Christ had only twelve?" Without access to the Scriptures, it was nearly impossible to question the legitimacy of the clergy's decisions.

Although we have Scripture today, I don't think we're too far from the same level of biblical illiteracy. The Catholic church was clergy-controlled, but today's church is pastor-dependent.

There was a three-year period when I stopped listening to podcasts of pastors preaching. The biggest trigger for my podcast fast was how pastor-dependent I had become. When I was writing a paper, preaching a text, or dialoguing with friends over a hot topic, I realized I almost always quoted a pastor before I quoted the Bible. Worse, I felt far more versed in pastors' opinions than in Scripture. Isn't that ironic? To be well *versed* in pastors' opinions? But I was. I could tell you five pastors' thoughts, four sermon jams, three good books, two new blogs, and a podcast in a pear tree. I was steeped in others' thought but hardly as confident in what *I* actually thought, or most important, what God has to say about a topic.

I don't think I'm alone in this. Whether we like it or not, we're in an era when churches are built around personality and popularity. We'll change churches for a better teacher. We'll build satellite campuses around great teachers. We get frustrated when there's a guest speaker. These are all signs of being pastor-dependent. Leonard Ravenhill once said, "The early church was married to poverty, prisons and persecutions. Today, the church is married to prosperity, personality, and popularity." Maybe it's time for a change?

READY for Reformation

	FIRST REFORMATION	NEXT REFORMATION
VIRAL VOICE	MASS PRINT	MASS MEDIA
BIBLICAL ILLITERACY	CLERGY-CONTROLLED	PASTOR-DEPENDENT
POWER TO THE PEOPLE	WORD	DISCIPLESHIP
CHURCH OUTCOME	THEOLOGY DIVIDES	MISSION UNITES

To think that clergy leaders once thought it was unwise to give people access to the Word of God. Erasmus, a Dutch theologian, couldn't stand this thinking. He said, "I absolutely dissent from those people who don't want the holy scriptures to be read in translation by the unlearned—as if, forsooth, Christ taught such a complex doctrine that hardly anyone outside a handful of theologians could understand it, or as if the chief strength of the Christian religion lay in people's ignorance of it. . . . I would hope that the farmer might chant a holy text at his plow, the spinner sing it as she sits at her wheel, the traveler ease the tedium of his journey with tales from the scripture. Let all conversation between Christians draw from this source."

> If the last reformation gave people the Word of God, I hope the next one gives us the work of God.

The same is happening with discipleship. We treat the congregation like they're not up for the task or it'll be too much for them. *We'll lose members. They're just not ready.* But the reality is, we were made for this. The church is in dire need of its mission.

If the last reformation divided the church, I hope the next one unites the church.

THE EVOLUTION OF CHURCH

SACRED EVENT

In the 1950s, church was a revered event our society insisted you attend. You put on your Sunday best, and you showed up to worship God. This was a nonnegotiable because it's what proper people did and because the church still held a place of authority within the culture. It may no longer have been the state religion that Constantine endorsed, but Christianity was still the moral voice of our country.

SACRED EVENT

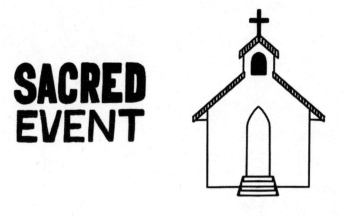

The image that comes to mind for me is Billy Graham praying beside presidents who sought him out for spiritual counsel and advice. There was nothing controversial about this. Even the phrase "wearing your Sunday best" evokes the idea of attending a sacred Sunday event. Back then a suit was the expectation, and now it's sort of extreme.

While not everyone who went to church surrendered their lives to God, it was seemingly a cultural obligation. You went to church because that's what you were supposed to do. It's what the vast majority of people did.

Then that changed.

SACRED AWESOME EVENT

Culture was changing, and soon the church would too. As the culture began to move in a more liberal direction, it slowly became more acceptable to skip out on church. The baby boomers had been dragged to church their entire lives, and now that they could decide whether they were going to attend, many chose not to. They had heard one too many hymns on the organ and more than enough stale sermons.

Attendance dipped. Something new needed to happen.

And it did.

Creative pastors showed up on the scene. They had new

ideas to reengage the next generation. Guys like Bill Hybels, Rick Warren, Andy Stanley, Ed Young, and Craig Groeschel (to name a few) founded churches that were not just sacred but also totally awesome. Culture was moving away from tradition, and the church could no longer count on social pressure to guide people toward it. Church needed to become more attractive to draw not only the beleaguered faithful but also those who were unchurched, or now dechurched. The model of "build it and they will come" could no longer be counted on to work.

A lot of people had been turned off by the simply sacred model. They wanted church to be something that looked more like what they were getting from other arenas of life. They wanted it to be fun, relational, and relevant.

The creative pastors came in and gave them just that. Cool worship bands replaced the large choirs. Topical talks replaced stodgy sermons. Pews were jettisoned for chairs with cupholders—for the drink you got, by the way, from the coffee shop that now existed *inside* your church.

It was a whole new world. Church was no longer just sacred. It was now sacred *and* it was awesome.

I want to be clear in saying the creative pastors didn't set out to make church less sacred. The gospel wasn't abandoned but rather repackaged in a way that caught the attention of society. To me, the church during this period mirrored the example of Paul, who strove to be all things to all people (1 Cor. 9:19–23).

This is how the seeker-sensitive church came about and then gave rise to the megachurch, a church that no longer looked like a traditional church but instead resembled a concert venue, adorned with a star pastor, stage lighting, cameras, smoke machines, and a rock band.

Not everyone liked this. A lot of Christians felt then, and many feel now, that this development did make church less sacred. Gone was the quiet reverence of the mass.

Regardless of whether this was right or wrong, churches did it and it worked.

The masses flowed through the doors, and many of these churches are still going strong today. My point in recounting this brief history is not to argue about whether this was a healthy development but just to say it happened.

I once was at a dinner with some young pastors, one of whom worked for Elevation Church in North Carolina. We were mostly joking around until somebody asked him about something we were all familiar with but never would dare ask about. She said, "I love Elevation Church, but some people give me a hard time for it. They say it's too seeker sensitive. Does it ever bother you when people label you guys that?" You could hear a pin drop as everyone waited for his answer. "No," he said. "It doesn't bother me. I mean, what's wrong with being seeker sensitive? Isn't that what Jesus came to do—seek and save the lost?"

It's hard to criticize a church that's trying to do what Jesus came to do. He's got a point I think we often forget. This is actually a little personal for me.

Growing up, I used to hate church. I never felt like I belonged when I was in church. I remember thinking, *You know what's worse than being all alone at home? Being all alone at church.* I hated feeling alone but surrounded by cliques of Christians who wouldn't include me. No one ever sought me out, until one day I walked through the doors of Fellowship Church in Grapevine, Texas. I didn't make it more than ten feet until I felt welcome. I wasn't just greeted, I was engaged. I was appreciated and included.

It was the first time I ever felt a sense of belonging in church. I gave my life to Christ that day.

> You know what's worse than being all alone at home? Being all alone at church.

I think we give these churches a hard time, when many in our cities came to know the Lord through them. Including myself. I wouldn't be writing this book today if churches were not sensitive to a seeker like me.

SACRED AWESOME AUTHENTIC EVENT

Then something happened. Younger generations were still attracted to the modern model of the seeker-sensitive church, but they wanted it to be a little less slick. They liked the quality production, the programming, and the relaxed atmosphere, but they needed to know their pastor wasn't too prim and proper.

This gave rise to pastors like Matt Chandler, Francis Chan, Mark Driscoll, and David Platt.

In some ways, their methods were anti–seeker sensitive. They were not interested in making the message easy to hear. They constantly pointed out the chasm between our hearts and God's Word. Whether they were yelling at you or weeping for you, each message was full of angst. Matt Chandler regularly gave what he called "space-making sermons." He knew that after he gave the message from the Scriptures, some people would probably leave the church. However, those who were looking for something raw

SACRED AWESOME AUTHENTIC EVENT

found a home in these churches. These messages would punch you in the soul, but people would want to come back for more. Even invite their friends. These messages revealed the heart of people and called them to repentance and a new way of living. There was a lot of truth, but also a lot of love, because they grew and grew. I think young men especially became attracted to these leaders because their preaching scratched an itch for a fatherless generation who didn't grow up with strong, raw, deeply devoted, Christ-following fathers. These pastors earned the right to convict by speaking the truth in love, like a father reproves a child whom he loves.

Another unique byproduct of these churches was some of their converts. It wasn't uncommon for a testimony to start with, "I've been going to church my whole life, but I've never realized the power of the gospel until now." The message engaged those who were dechurched, unchurched, and even overchurched.

Some of these churches, while large in size, eschewed the fancy trappings of the megachurches. The spaces were big, but the worship experience was a little simpler. There were fewer elaborate lighting systems, fewer smoke machines, and in the Village's case, no coffee shop in the lobby. Aesthetically and programmatically, they still looked similar to the megachurches that came before them, but they placed a deeper emphasis on community, hoping to make a large church feel smaller, so people could connect and hold one another accountable. There was a theme of raising the bar and being in your business. Being a member had a cost. But their people were willing to do church with fewer amenities and more accountability. Even if it hurt sometimes, they knew it'd be helpful in the long run.

SACRED AWESOME AUTHENTIC DISCIPLES

So where do we go from here?

Back to the beginning, I hope. We need to look at our past to reach our future. In the beginning, the church was all about sending out disciples. There was no sacred event to even speak of. Jesus brought his disciples together, taught them, spent time with them, and then sent them out. This is what the church needs to be doing. If you look at these models, which one looks closest to the early church?

Of course, we will come together on Sunday and worship God, as we should, but I believe we need to shift our focus from Sunday morning worship out into the rest of the week. The major shift in this model is from building up an event to building up disciples. Have you ever considered that when you ask someone, "How was church?" they usually tell you one of two things? They say either, "The message was great!" or, "Worship was great!" Church has been dwindled down to two people doing two things for about two hours. That's pretty crazy! What about everyone else? Everybody gets 168 hours in their week. Our strongest members spend five to eight hours at church, at best. But we spend most of our lives

at work. Studies show that a third of our lives will be spent at work (92,120 hours). It sounds like *that* should be our mission field and the place where we equip our people. Sunday should always be a priority, but I don't think we can ever make disciples as Jesus wants us to if Sunday morning is the be-all and end-all. In this model, church is less of an event and more of a pit stop.

> Church has been dwindled down to two people doing two things for about two hours.

In racing, a pit stop is a place to refuel and get back in the race. However, the right pit crew is needed to quickly and effectively build up the body of believers and send them to the racetrack equipped and ready.

CHAPTER 10, "PIT CREW PASTORS"

The pastor of this church doesn't wake up and ask himself, "How is my church?"

He wakes up and asks himself, "How is my city?"

He believes that it's not that God's church has a mission but that God's mission has a church.

If you start with the health of the church, it'll never be good. So you'll focus internally. But if you start with the health of the city, you'll see the church as a means to meet the needs of the city. The church will become an instrument rather than an event.

> Church should be less of an event and more of a pit stop.

When you consider the welfare of your city and not just the welfare of your members, you realize the gravity of need around you. In turn, you realize the necessity for unity. I remember asking Tim Keller about this, and as usual he had a mic-drop answer. I asked him, "Being as busy as you are with your own ministry, why do you, as a senior pastor, make so much time to unify and equip other local churches in New York?" He replied, "In the church body, growth that does not benefit the rest of the body is not biblical. In the human body, cells that benefit only themselves are called cancer."

Surely, we don't have the audacity to believe we can fulfill as one church what Jesus proclaimed for *the* church? I'm not saying neglect the body. I'm saying embrace the city. If you really think about it, if Jesus had started each day asking, "How are the Twelve?" he'd never have gotten to do what he came to do, and the Twelve never would have become who they were designed to be.

I wonder if that's true of us all.

THE FOUR STAGES OF GOD'S RELATIONSHIP WITH MAN

1. *God* and *us*. Adam and Eve walked naked in the garden with God. They had no shame. God and man lived in

perfect harmony with one another. Unfortunately, this was short-lived.

2. *God* for *us*. After the fall, man couldn't be in the presence of God. God, however, sent guidance. Whether he did it through prophets, judges, commandments, or covenants, God was still for us.

3. *God* with *us*. Then God took the form of man. He sent his Son to preach the good news and call people home. His Son was born in Bethlehem, and his name was Immanuel, "God with us."

4. *God* in *us*. As Jesus predicted, the temple was later destroyed (in AD 70). Fortunately, God's presence was no longer bound to a temple or accessed through a high priest. Jesus put an end to animal sacrifices when he became our sacrificial lamb. The temple's curtain was torn. The altar closed. *And the temple was multiplied.* The cross of Jesus changed the church. God moved from being for us, to being with us, to being *in* us. The Bible says, "Christ in you [is] the hope of glory" (Col. 1:27).

This idea of God being in us is laced throughout the New Testament.

- First Corinthians 6:19 says, "Do you not know that your bodies are temples of the Holy Spirit, who is in you, whom you have received from God?"
- Second Timothy 1:14 says, "Guard the good deposit that was entrusted to you—guard it with the help of the Holy Spirit who lives in us."
- Galatians 2:20 says, "I have been crucified with Christ and I no longer live, but Christ lives in me."

All these verses point to one revolutionary idea. The church is no longer a place. It's now a people. Wherever we are, there the church is. Basically, Christians turn buildings into churches. Churches don't turn people into Christians.

I love how Watermark Community Church puts it. With the rise of satellite campuses, many megachurches will say something like, "We are one church in three locations." But Watermark says they are "one church, three campuses, thousands of locations." They view their building as the facility and their people as the church.

> Wherever we are, there the church is.

How you view God's church changes how you view God's mission. And vice versa.

According to the Barna Group, 71 percent of Christians say the main influence in their salvation was not going to church but a personal relationship with a Christian.[14] This is so important for us to recognize, because this generation doesn't trust institutions. But they will trust someone who *represents* one.

Things have changed in this generation. Young people don't read the Bible. They read Christians. It's why I care about this new model of church for millennials and Gen Zers. Although they may not be going to the event on Sunday, they are meeting Christians throughout the week. They're meeting us at their job, in their neighborhood, in their daily rhythms. We have ambassadors all over the world. Many are like those special agents in *The Bourne Identity*. They're dormant, casually living their lives, waiting for their assignment, not realizing all that's within them. The problem is most churches are strong at gathering and weak at scattering. Barna found that within two years of conversion, 80 percent of Christians give up their former friendships with unbelievers. We subtly construct holy huddles. We become comfortable with the ninety-nine and forget the one.

Remember, the Bible says, "How beautiful are the feet of those who bring good news" (Rom. 10:15). Not, "How beautiful are the churches we bring people to." When we shift our focus from creating great temple experiences to training Great Commission disciples, we leverage the full benefits of the cross. After giving us his commission, Jesus said, "Surely I am with you always" (Matt.

28:20). So God is with us, because God is in us. Do people in the pews live like this? What a shame if they don't realize it's "through the church [that] the manifold wisdom of God should be made known" (Eph. 3:10).

5. *God* and *us.* One day Christ will return and all things will be made new. God and man, back in harmony. What a redemption story! The beautiful irony is that there is a fifth stage, which is simply a return to the first stage. This is good news. This is worth sharing.

> The Bible says, "How beautiful are the feet of those who bring good news." Not, "How beautiful are the churches we bring people to."

"HOW *Beautiful* ARE THE **FEET** of THOSE WHO BRING **GOOD NEWS.** **NOT** "HOW *Beautiful* ARE THE **CHURCHES** WE BRING THEM TO."

GOD *and* US — THE GARDEN

GOD *for* US — THE OLD TESTAMENT

GOD *with* US — THE GOSPELS

GOD *in* US — NOW!

CHURCH SHOULD BE LESS of AN EVENT AND MORE of A LAUNCHING PAD

the last Reformation GAVE PEOPLE THE WORD of GOD, THE NEXT ONE WILL GIVE THEM the WORK of GOD

PART 2

WHAT MILLENNIALS LOOK FOR IN CHURCH

THE FIVE POSITIONS
ON A DREAM TEAM

I n 1992, the best basketball team to ever assemble made history. It was the first time we saw so many household names on one team, because it was the first time NBA players were able to play in the Olympics. *Sports Illustrated* called them the Dream Team, and it stuck. Just to get an idea of how good this team was, of the twelve players on the team, eleven of them are in the Hall of Fame.

1992 OLYMPIC DREAM TEAM ROSTER

Michael Jordan: shooting guard
Magic Johnson: point guard
Larry Bird: small forward
Charles Barkley: power forward
Patrick Ewing: center
David Robinson: center
Clyde Drexler: shooting guard
John Stockton: point guard
Karl Malone: power forward
Chris Mullin: shooting guard
Scottie Pippen: small forward
Christian Laettner: small forward

The Dream Team was unstoppable! But there's one thing most people don't know about them.

They lost their very first game. Worse, they lost to some college kids.

Their first scrimmage was against the nonprofessional college athletes who would have gone to the Olympics if NBA players hadn't been allowed that year. The college team had some good players, but nothing compared with the Dream Team. I bet most people don't even know the name of the leading scorer, who embarrassed the Dream Team. The most dominant player, who shut down Jordan, Magic, and Bird, was none other than six foot, 165 pound Bobby Hurley.

Probably not what you were expecting.

After the game, Magic Johnson said, "We didn't know how to play with each other. So these young kids were killing us." Larry Bird even said in an interview after the scrimmage, "Some of these college kids we just got done playing should probably be on this team."

Some theorize that Coach Daly purposely sabotaged the game so these all-star athletes would know they weren't untouchable. He didn't want the Dream Team to take their competition lightly. One thing is for sure. Some of the best basketball players to ever play the game were on a court with some college kids who were just excited to play with their heroes, later to find out they actually beat their heroes.

So what's my point? Here it is. It doesn't matter how great the players are if they don't know how to play as a team. The team wasn't lacking talent. It was lacking unity.

> We don't lack talent. We lack unity.

Isn't this true of our leaders in the church today? We have some of the most gifted leaders in the world, but we're not unified. We have people with various talents, but we seem to leverage only a few of them. We've been given the Dream Team, but we're letting the world beat us like some college kids.

I want to focus on a disunity in our leadership that is fundamentally structuring churches to miss millennials. It's probably not what you think. There are a lot of divisions in the church, but the one I'm going to talk about doesn't get talked about much, and I've never seen someone tie the implications to millennials.

So what division am I talking about? Not racial division. Not denominational division. Not even generational division. I want to share the implications of occupational division.

Unity isn't everyone doing the same thing. It's everyone doing different things in the same direction. But in the church, the only way you feel like you're doing real ministry is if you work in vocational ministry. This has to change.

LEADERSHIP ROLES IN THE CHURCH

The church is going to have to reevaluate the roles of people in the church who are not in "ministry positions." I'm reminded of a sentiment that is often attributed to Martin Luther. He said the Christian cobbler doesn't fulfill his Christian duty by putting little crosses on every pair of shoes he makes but rather fulfills his duty by making the best pair of shoes he possibly can.

Paul calls the church to be unified. He says we are to be of "one body and one Spirit" (Eph. 4:4). As followers of Jesus, we have all been given grace to be humble, gentle, patient, and able to bear with one another in love (v. 2). We need to be one. But a body has many parts, and God has given the leaders of the church different roles to play. Christ has appointed "the apostles, the prophets, the evangelists, the pastors and teachers, to equip his people for works of service, so that the body of Christ may be built up until we all reach unity in the faith and in the knowledge of the Son of God and become mature, attaining to the whole measure of the fullness of Christ" (Eph. 4:11–13).

To better understand what kind of church millennials are looking for and need, let's take a look at each kind of leader that Paul describes in Ephesians. Apostles, prophets, and evangelists know the gospel. They love the gospel. They are all about the gospel. But they are more interested in communicating the gospel to the culture than to the church. Shepherds and teachers also love the gospel, but they are better equipped for and more focused on teaching and caring for the church body than taking the gospel to the rest of the world. The church needs all five types of leaders.

> Apostles, prophets, and evangelists usually focus on the culture, while shepherds and teachers mostly focus on the church.

To keep them all straight, I like to use the acronym APEST for apostles, prophets, evangelists, shepherds, and teachers. This is how it looks when I put it up on a whiteboard.

Because the church is more familiar with the roles of shepherd and teacher, let's start there.

TEACHERS

In my opinion, this is the most common gifting of a senior pastor. Over the last few decades, the most successful pastors have been those who are very gifted teachers. These are men and women who are able to go up to the pulpit and preach a lights-out sermon. Whether they're inspirational or instructional, they're able to make really complex biblical truths simple.

A teacher is someone who can read the Word of God and understand it in such a way that he or she can correct others' misunderstandings of Scripture. They shine light on truth, and they shine light on bad teaching.

You know that saying people use whenever the word *therefore* comes up in the Bible? Whenever you see therefore, go back to see what it's there for. We can thank our teacher brothers and sisters who constantly remind us.

A teacher is a person who will study theology and then help explain that theology to the rest of the church.

A teacher gets fired up about studying the Bible. A teacher views spending time in the Word not as a burden but rather as the primary activity that gives them energy and strength and excitement. Teachers love the Bible so much, they are not satisfied to read it in English alone; they appreciate learning Hebrew and Greek so they can read the original manuscripts themselves!

It's all about clarity. Poor theology can lead to poor obedience. Unlike the evangelist, a teacher is going to direct most of his or her time and energy inward, to the church. A teacher will notice something in a passage that you've never noticed all your life. They see the nuances that make a big difference. They defend the truth and equip us with it.

POTENTIAL TEACHER WEAKNESSES

- They can become judgmental, always correcting people's theology.
- They can become puffed up with knowledge.
- They can surround themselves with only Christians.

WELL-KNOWN TEACHERS

Tony Evans
John MacArthur
Beth Moore
Robert Morris
J. I. Packer
John Piper
R. C. Sproul
N. T. Wright

SHEPHERDS

A shepherd is someone who is always willing to take time and listen to the troubles of another person.

Shepherds don't have the "fix it" mindset of the apostle and the evangelist. Shepherds understand that sometimes the need is not to fix a situation but rather to tend to it. So they will care for people by listening to them without trying to fix them.

Shepherds are trustworthy, which is why people are so comfortable sharing their troubles with them. They don't have personalities that easily offend but are usually calm and soft-spoken.

Shepherds are the glue of most ministries because they are the constant, steadying voice of compassion and wisdom. They are not quickly angered or knocked off course.

A shepherd enjoys spending time with the people most others reject. Like the Good Shepherd himself, the shepherd will leave the flock of sheep behind to go out of his way to find the one who is lost. Shepherds are great at noticing who is left out and on the margins, and they will do all in their power to include this person and make them feel loved. This requires lots of patience, which the shepherd also has.

> Shepherds are the beating heart that is most missed when absent.

Shepherds provide the why for ministry. They are the beating heart that is most missed when absent. Because they bless and encourage people, they provide a gravitas that is most often not fully appreciated until it is gone. Healthy ministries must have shepherds.

POTENTIAL SHEPHERD WEAKNESSES

- They can overprogram spiritual growth, becoming dependent on routine and predictability.
- They can insulate their flock, not allowing them to become lambs among wolves.
- They can nurture a culture that allows people to become codependent on them.

WELL-KNOWN SHEPHERDS

Brené Brown
Bob Goff

kingdom connectors. Again, Paul is a great example of this. He's such a networker, constantly name-dropping. Don't believe me? Read Romans 16, and you'll see the most name-dropping since the family lineage chapters in the Bible. Paul seemed to know everyone. He's always mentioning someone in his letters. It's the nature of apostles.

Fortunately, healthy apostles can celebrate when others win, because they know that their vision is too big to accomplish alone. So they lean toward collaboration.

POTENTIAL APOSTLE WEAKNESSES

- They can easily get anxious, bored, and/or frustrated.
- They can have opinions about everything and how it should be done.
- They can sometimes be intimidating, not easily approachable, and/or hard to read.

WELL-KNOWN APOSTLES

Jennie Allen
Mark Burnett
Christine Caine
Louie Giglio
Craig Groeschel
Chris Hodges
Brian Houston
Tim Keller
T. D. Jakes
John Maxwell

PROPHETS

Similar to the prophets of the Bible, the current-day prophet is somebody who knows the truth and then challenges the public and the people of God with that truth. A prophet can take the message of God and convict people to do something about that message. A prophet is unafraid to passionately declare God's truth in any and all situations, regardless of the consequences. Sharing, for them, isn't about the platform; it's about the burden. Prophets don't just teach what you should believe or not believe. They have a tendency to punch you in the stomach with it.

In the words of J. R. Woodward, prophets are "heart revealers." They have a way to view our actions, discern our motives, and reveal our hearts. The work of a prophet takes a special kind of person with a special kind of courage, because most of us don't want to hear what is in our hearts. A prophet is willing to look us in the eye and tell us. This is Nathan with David. This is Samuel with Saul.

We trust the prophet to do this, because what a prophet does first and foremost is take time to listen to God. We don't just take a prophet at his word because we think he is really smart. We take a prophet at his word because we believe he listens to the One who knows all. A prophet brings a message from God, not his own message. There is power in this kind of weight, but there is also a unique type of loneliness. It's difficult when your job is to tell people to change, and you seem to be the only one who cares. This is conjecture, but I think that weighed on Jonah a ton more than he is given credit for.

Francis Chan is a great example of someone who isn't so much preaching as pleading. He doesn't just want us to learn something. He wants us to change. He really wants us to repent. He's spent time with the Father, and he wants us to have that same level of intimacy.

▶ Chapter 11, "Francis Chan Prophet Impersonation"

Matt Chandler comes to mind when I think of a prophet. If you don't know, Chandler is the pastor of the Village Church. He's a no-nonsense, dynamic preacher who has done really well with millennials. But it's not because he is warm and fuzzy. Chandler regularly preaches what he calls "space-making sermons." These are sermons that he knows will open up space in his church because people will leave after hearing them. He doesn't usually tell his church what they want to hear; he tells them what they need to hear. These are sermons filled with hard truths that a lot of pastors would avoid in an effort not to offend anyone. But Chandler, like all prophets, isn't primarily concerned with making people happy or comfortable where they are. Instead prophets show us where we need to be. Prophets do not shy away from the challenge of the gospel or the call to repentance. Nor do they back down from speaking truth to people in power.

POTENTIAL PROPHET WEAKNESSES

- They can sometimes deliver their needed message with all truth and no love.
- They can die on a hill for something that's preference and not "thus says the Lord."
- They can struggle with loneliness, feeling that no one else cares like they care.

WELL-KNOWN PROPHETS

Jeff Bethke
Francis Chan
Matt Chandler
Rich Mullins
Jen Hatmaker
Martin Luther King Jr.
Lecrae
Martin Luther
Eric Mason
Propaganda

EVANGELISTS

The evangelist is the person who is always pestering the rest of us about when we are going to get off our butts and do something about whatever problem we are facing. Whether it's unemployment or disease or finding Joseph Kony in Uganda, an evangelist will not sit back and let others solve the problem. An evangelist must go and pitch in.

An evangelist cannot sit still for as long as it takes to accomplish the task. They must go, go, go!

The evangelist is never content doing work inside the four walls of the church. If you told them 99 percent of their work would be only with Christians, it would make them cringe. They will of course do work in the church, but their heart is fed by going outside the church. They truly have a heart for the unreached and overlooked, locally and/or globally.

Evangelists are antagonists who poke and prod the leaders around them because they are filled with urgency. This urgency will often lead them to leave the church and start a nonprofit if they feel like it is a more efficient way to solve the problem or meet the need.

Evangelists often have better relationships with non-Christians than with Christians. These people are constantly rubbing shoulders with unbelievers. For them, it's not really strategic. It's just natural.

My friend and rapper Street Hymns is an evangelist. Street voluntarily lives in one of the most dangerous neighborhoods in Dallas. He regularly hears gunfire and witnesses violence, and he has been told repeatedly by well-meaning Christians that he needs to move out of the apartment complex he is in. Since he easily can afford to live in a better part of town, why doesn't he? Why put himself at risk? He'll tell you it's because if he leaves, he's not sure who is going to minister to the people who are left behind. "I can leave the ghetto," he once told me, "but my neighbors can't. So I'm staying and telling people about Jesus through my music."

That's an evangelist.

Evangelists are unafraid of sharing the gospel, no matter the circumstances. They may not always be great speakers, but they will get the message across with words, actions, and their lives. For them, sharing the gospel isn't something they do; it's who they are. God's story has changed their story.

Evangelists can sometimes be wild cards or downright interesting people. They are renegades like Todd White or David Platt or William Carey. Their gospel-motivated life choices can sometimes be so radical that they aren't easily understood. These guys are all about the mission, and they might make other people feel uncomfortable in the process.

I lived with some evangelists when the Ebola virus hit near our apartments in Dallas a few years ago. I don't know if you have ever been near an Ebola outbreak, but I can tell you this: nobody wants to be close to that. When helicopters are flying over your apartment complex 24/7 and you look on the national news to see your neighborhood, you wonder if maybe you should do a guys' night at someone else's home for a while. Everyone wants to get as far away as possible, for obvious reasons. My roommates, however, were trying to get into the apartments! It was crazy. They just really wanted to help in any way they could. That's why they wanted to live in Vickery Meadow to begin with, to love refugees. They were all over it. That, to me, epitomizes the heart of an evangelist. They want to go to wherever the action is, no matter what the cost.

> Evangelists can't help but share how God's story changed their story.

C. T. Studd had a saying that can sum up the heart of an evangelist: "Some want to live within the sound of church or chapel bell; I want to run a rescue shop, within a yard of hell."

POTENTIAL EVANGELIST WEAKNESSES

- They might guilt and shame people into mission instead of gracefully guiding them.
- They can become very bitter and impatient toward the church, using them for funding but internally bashing the Bride.
- They can remove themselves so much from other believers that they become unrelatable and therefore they're unable to recruit new missionaries.

WELL-KNOWN EVANGELISTS

Reinhard Bonnke
William Carey
Todd White
Elisabeth Elliot
J. John
Billy Graham
Greg Laurie
Carl Lentz
David Platt

In this process, you may have seen one or two that strongly identify with your gifting. We're usually strong in one or two and weaker in the rest. I like this because it requires us to lean on each other as the body. Only Jesus was the perfect apostle, the perfect prophet, the perfect evangelist, the perfect shepherd, and the perfect teacher. He is the embodiment of it all. Ephesians 4 goes on to say that we should "grow to become in every respect the mature body of him who is the head, that is, Christ. From him the whole body, joined and held together by every supporting ligament, grows and builds itself up in love, as each part does its work."

But here's the problem. Many times we treat these giftings like they're reserved for the Old and New Testaments. This limits and underequips the body. A speaker recently commented on this at a gathering of apostolic leaders.[15] You can see his work on the next page.

DREAM TEAM UNIFIED

After their loss, the Dream Team got their act together. And once they were on the same page, they dominated anyone and everyone in their way. They ended up having a rematch the next day against the college team that beat them. This time they were unified.

And this time they won by more than a hundred points.

But they didn't stop there. In their first official game to qualify

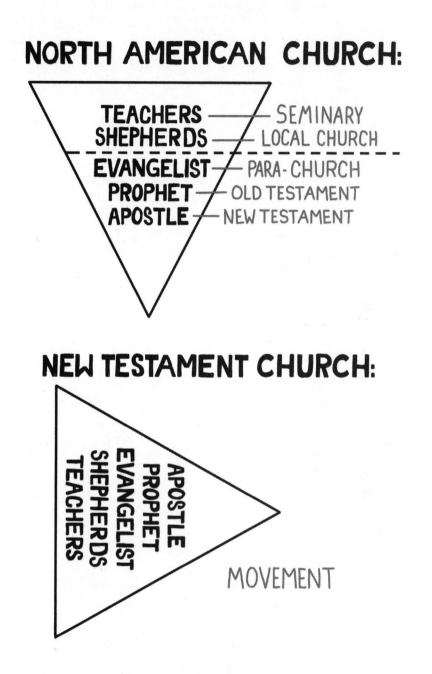

NORTH AMERICAN CHURCH:

TEACHERS ——— SEMINARY
SHEPHERDS ——— LOCAL CHURCH
- -
EVANGELIST —— PARA-CHURCH
PROPHET —— OLD TESTAMENT
APOSTLE —— NEW TESTAMENT

NEW TESTAMENT CHURCH:

APOSTLE
PROPHET
EVANGELIST
SHEPHERDS
TEACHERS

MOVEMENT

for the Olympics, they defeated Cuba by seventy-nine points, 136 to 57. The commentator of the game later said, "It was as if [the Americans] were playing a high school team, or grade school team." The Cuban team never stood a chance.

The Dream Team had some of the best point guards, shooting guards, small forwards, power forwards, and centers in the world. They won every game in the Olympics by an average of forty points. If that's what they could do with five unified roles in the Olympics, imagine what we could do with five unified roles in the church?

Now that we know the implications of occupational disunity, let's ask the more intriguing question: What does this have to do with millennials? You'll see in the next chapter.

We don't **LACK TALENT**

We LACK UNITY

UNITY ISN'T EVERYONE DOING the SAME THING

IT'S EVERYONE DOING **DIFFERENT** THINGS _in the_ **SAME** DIRECTION.

POOR theology CAN LEAD TO POOR obedience

THE DREAM TEAM:

APOSTLES 00

PROPHETS 00

EVANGELISTS 00

SHEPHERDS 00

TEACHERS 00

CHAPTER 12

WHY MILLENNIALS
SUPPORT CAUSES BUT
NOT THE CHURCH

In 2014, *Christianity Today* made a list of thirty-three of the most influential Christians under the age of thirty-three.[16] The following is just a sample of the names, but I want you to pay close attention to what type of influencers made the list.

Jeff Bethke: YouTube personality
Esther Havens: international photographer
Nick Vujicic: inspirational speaker born without arms or legs
Lila Rose: pro-life activist
Joshua DuBois: Barack Obama's faith adviser
Nabeel Qureshi: former Muslim apologist
Daniel Kolenda: evangelist to millions
Salomon Ligthelm: filmmaker, designer, musician
Trip Lee: rapper, author, pastor
Christena Cleveland: racial reconciliation advocate
Dale Partridge: entrepreneur for good

All of these influential Christians are doing ministry, but none of them are full-time pastors. Of the thirty-three, only a handful are ordained pastors. I think this is significant because it signals the new way millennials are willing to see ministry. No longer does a person need to have an ecclesiastical title for young people to see them as a legitimate Christian authority. It also reveals who will be the influencers of the next generation. These are mostly apostolic, prophetic, and evangelistic leaders. Or we can call them APEs!

Now, just think about the senior pastors who have deeply connected with millennials over the last ten years. Many of them are prophets far more than they are teachers. There are guys like Matt Chandler, Francis Chan, David Platt, and Todd White. The common denominator is that these men aren't really preaching. They're pleading. Their message cuts straight to the heart and leaves you with a knot in your stomach. They are calling us to repentance, with truth and love. We need that. It hurts so good. But young adults keep coming back for more.

But check this out. There's been a shift of some senior pastors doing the unthinkable, leaving their church. Here are a few APE leaders who have left serving *a* church so they can better serve *the* church.

- Francis Chan leaves Cornerstone Community Church and considers becoming a missionary in China but decides to start a church-planting network in San Francisco.
- David Platt leaves the Church at Brook Hills so he can help launch missionaries across the globe through the International Mission Board. (I think he's a mix of teacher and evangelist, because in the middle of my writing this, he has decided to go back to teaching. However, it's clear that he's torn between the two roles. And can still do both as a teacher-pastor.)
- Timothy Keller leaves Redeemer Presbyterian Church to better equip and mobilize new church plants in major cities around the globe.

When Francis Chan was asked why he'd give up such a great church he helped start, he answered, "It was time for me to go. It was bothering me that people were quoting Francis Chan more than Jesus Christ." This sounds like a man who doesn't just want to be a teaching pastor but also wants to be a missionary.

When Timothy Keller was thanked for his ministry and encouraged for his faithfulness as he retired, Keller quickly responded, "I'm not retiring. I'm moving into a strategic role of raising up leaders and training the next generation." That sounds like an apostle to me. That sounds like someone who's going to leverage his platform and wisdom to maximize the potential of the next generation of church planters.

Even guys like Matt Chandler are able to remain in their role as senior pastor but also find outlets to express the fullness of their gifting. Chandler is a great Bible teacher. No doubt about it. More important, however, Chandler has an apostolic and prophetic gifting. A lot of people openly questioned how Chandler could balance shepherding his church, preaching all over the world, and taking on the presidency of Acts 29 (a church-planting network). I think it's because Acts 29 doesn't burden him. It blesses him. I believe it gives him life. Apostles thrive when they get to lead other leaders. Chandler has made quite a few apostolic decisions at the Village that have pioneered some innovative ways of doing church. One of the most recent is turning satellite campuses into fully functioning church plants. That's almost unheard of. But apostles thrive in the unknown. My guess is this will become the norm in ten years.

Other senior pastors who have an APE gifting and have found an outlet toward the culture are guys like Carl Lentz, Judah Smith, and Rich Wilkerson. These pastors have been criticized for their influence on celebrities, but I bet that their whole lives, they've had influence with the influencers. It's in their God-given DNA. They're a mix of evangelist and prophet. The platforms are just larger now with the people they're impacting. Whether it's Judah Smith mentoring Justin Bieber, Carl Lentz befriending Kevin Durant, or Rich Wilkerson officiating at Kanye West's wedding, God has given them a Joseph-like seat with influencers who shape the culture. I'm thankful for it.

Last, I want to point out guys like Jeff Bethke, Propaganda, and Lecrae. Bethke and Propaganda became very well known after their spoken word videos attracted millions of views on YouTube. For those unfamiliar with spoken word, think passionate poetry. Jeff Bethke of course is known for his video "Why I Hate Religion but Love Jesus," and Propaganda for "The Gospel in Four Minutes." Follow me here. I think media like YouTube, and even hip-hop, are being used as a platform for prophets to speak to this next generation. I mean, go YouTube the song "Church Clothes" by Lecrae and tell me it doesn't have a prophetic message in there. He's not looking for you to dance. He's looking for you to respond.

CHAPTER 12, "ARTISTIC PROPHETS"

All these APEs "coincidentally" are very influential among millennials. The problem is that while millennials are more attracted to APEs (apostles, prophets, and evangelists), the church has mostly been led by shepherds and teachers. I mean, which one sounds more like millennials to you, the group that wants to go out into the world to change the culture or the group that wants to mostly stay in among Christians?

> Millennials are tired of hearing about Acts but not seeing them.

Instead of admiring great preachers, millennials are far more likely to see non-profit leaders, business leaders, artists, church planters, and online influencers as their role models. Remember, this is a generation who's tired of hearing about Acts but not seeing them. They are drawn to pastors who desire to be in the community, not just at their pulpit.

SEMINARY: A SAFE HAVEN FOR SHEPHERDS AND TEACHERS

When I first went to seminary, I thought I would be there with a bunch of world changers. You've got to realize that I was very new to the faith when I went to seminary, so I didn't know what to expect. My high school didn't have many Christians, so I was excited to finally be around others who wanted to take the gospel to the hardest places in our city.

But it turns out, more than trying to reach the lost, my seminary friends wanted to solve the mysteries of the universe. Are you Calvinist or Arminian? Because you better not say you're *just* a Christian! Honest to God, I'd never heard of this conversation until I got to seminary. But luckily, I got to hear about it from then on out. Every. Single. Day.

Now, don't get me wrong. I valued my experience there. I was so wet behind the ears. I didn't know anything about church history. I didn't know anything about theology. But I started falling in love with the old dead dudes. Charles Spurgeon, George Mueller, C. T. Studd, Martin Luther, Andrew Murray, William Wilberforce, C. S. Lewis, and Augustine, to name a few. To this day, I prefer two types of books. I like Christian books by old dead guys because they have a type of angst I just don't see in many modern Christian books. I also like business books that make the bestseller list, because I believe all truth is God's truth. These business leaders have stumbled onto principles God has already given us. I want the angst from our forefathers but the insight of our modern thought leaders. Models change. The message doesn't.

My seminary friends didn't agree. They'd question me, saying, "How can you read a book on Steve Jobs? He's not even a Christian!" And oh man, did they give me a hard time for reading *How to Win Friends and Influence People.* "What type of sorcery is this?" they'd say. At least that's what I heard in my head. The secular-and-sacred divide became very clear to me in seminary.

But I think it's deeper than just some things being sacred and some things being secular. I think we have leanings in the way God has designed us. And unfortunately for me, I was reading apostolic business books in a shepherd and teacher safe haven—seminary.

Don't just believe me. Try this. I've done it dozens of times, and it never fails. Ask someone you know in seminary this question: How many students do you know at the seminary who are . . .

- spending most their time off campus with unbelievers?
- entrepreneurial with a lucrative business?
- sometimes critical toward the students' lack of evangelism?
- gifted musicians who are getting a lot of attention mostly from unbelievers?

Whenever I ask these questions, they have to think hard just to name a few fellow students described this way. Then ask them this: How many students do you know at your seminary who are . . .

- very gifted at breaking down the Scriptures in ways people can understand?
- great listeners and discerning in the biblical counsel they should give?
- well read, studious, and almost like an encyclopedia on God's truth?
- sometimes critical toward churches with "bad" theology?

Every time they'll answer something to the effect of, "*Everyone at my school is good at these!*" Case and point. Seminary was designed to equip pastors for the church. And that's great. More so, it's needed.

But here's the problem. This generation isn't going to church! So the most equipped leaders are the least effective, and the least equipped leaders don't even see their work as worship. Most Christians with "real" jobs don't feel like they're doing real ministry.

> I know seminaries train pastors for the church. But we need to train missionaries for the city.

I know seminaries train pastors for the church. But we need to train missionaries for the city. That's where the young people are.

Our seminaries and churches must take note of this, because the marketplace is the mission field for millennials.

By the way, we're already seeing churches respond to the narrow training of seminaries. Notice that churches don't hire seminary students like they used to. Many of the larger churches that are reaching the next generation mostly hire from within. Or better, they're creating their own residency program or theological training courses, which serve as a precursor for whom they may hire. If you really think about it, Jesus strategically did the same. Have you ever considered that Jesus didn't choose one single religious leader to be a part of the Twelve? No scribe, no Pharisee, no Sadducee. Just twelve people from the marketplace—twelve uneducated, common men who were bold because they had been with the Lord.

(P.S. There's a place for both pastors for the church and missionaries for the city. If there ever was a man who shouldn't doubt that God loves him, it's Paul. I mean, bro, Jesus came back one more time just for you! Jesus strategically leveraged Paul, a religious leader, and when Paul joined the disciples, they made quite an impact together. Ironically, in all God's humor, the religious leader ended up getting a "real" job, tentmaking, and the fishermen ended up being too busy with their ministry to wait on tables for widows. Maybe there's more common ground in our work than we think!)

We Need More APEs

Paul said that we should be regarded as "stewards of the mysteries of God" (1 Cor. 4:1 ESV). I love that title! I think all Christians should be regarded as stewards of the mysteries of God. However, too often we believe that only ordained ministers are stewards of the mysteries of God. Worse yet, we believe ministry happens only in the church. And in our focus on the church, we neglect whole swathes of culture that need our presence: business, the arts, media, politics, sports, science, and education, just to name a few.

This tension and divide between clergy and layperson, between church and culture, has to go. If the church wants to reach the next generation, it has to allow more apostles, prophets, and evangelists to lead and influence the direction of the church. This inevitably will move the body from a church-focused mindset to a culture-focused outlook. The apostles, prophets, and evangelists think externally, which is where the young people are. When we keep our people inside, we reject culture, but when we disperse our people, we redeem it. Maybe even create it. There was a day when Christians created culture. (Now we just seem to copy it.) Our faith influenced the birth of hospitals, universities, and even this country. I bet you didn't know that 106 of America's first 108 colleges were started as Christian institutions.

> You don't get labeled a "friend of sinners" if most of your time is spent in the church.

I like to remind people that Jesus, during the course of his ministry, performed around forty miracles. Most of them happened outside the temple. The same goes for his disciples. Of the forty miracles in Acts, only one happened in the temple. You don't get labeled a "friend of sinners" if most of your time is spent in the church.

The mantra of shepherds and teachers leans toward "Come as you are."

The mantra of apostles, prophets, and evangelists leans toward "Go where they are."

Which one sounds more like the mantra of this generation? Honestly, both. They're inclusive and adventurous. So what if we changed it to "Go as you are"? Wherever God has you, be all there. It reminds me of Matthew 10:7: "As you go, preach" (NASB). Steward the mysteries of God exactly where God has placed you. If you are a scientist, do careful research in the context of learning and caring for God's creation. If you are an athlete, compete with self-discipline, resilience, and integrity. If you are a business owner, make high-quality products while serving the dignity of both your customer and your employees.

Shepherds and teachers tend to want younger people to come in and serve the church, giving up their outside activities. But pastors need to understand that the more you empower young people to go serve outside the church, the more they will be inspired to come and serve inside the church.

> If your church closed its doors, how long would it take for the neighborhood to notice?

The test for gauging whether your church is internally or externally focused is a simple question. If your church closed its doors, how long would it take for the neighborhood to notice?

A week? A month? A year? Would the neighborhood ever notice? And if they did, would they care? This is how a millennial thinks. It's a very practical question because it's a very practical generation.

How Churches Can Value APEs

How can a church communicate to millennials that it will be a place that values the apostles, prophets, and evangelists? Here are a few ideas.

1. REMOVE THEIR GUILT

Byron Sanders is a bright young leader in Dallas. He is deeply passionate about the Dallas Independent School District, for which he advocates tirelessly in an effort to provide students with the best possible mentors and resources for their education. He's just one of those guys who has his hands in a lot of civic matters around town, always trying to make Dallas the best city it can be. In fact, if you told me Byron would someday be the mayor of Dallas, I would not be surprised at all. He also happens to be a committed Christian who sometimes feels guilty for not being involved in church as much as he'd like to be.

Thankfully, his pastor, Bryan Carter, the senior pastor of Concord Church, did one of the best things he could have done. One day Byron and Bryan were talking, and Byron confessed that he felt guilty that he's so involved in the city and barely involved in the church. In a moment of vulnerability, Byron asked, "What can I do to better help the church with my gifting?"

In a surprise response, Pastor Carter said, "Keep doing what you're doing. You're doing things for the school district I could never do. And when you're out there, I see it as an extension of our church. In fact, you *are* serving the church when you serve the city. When you're serving Dallas schools, you're telling the city that our church cares."

Pastor Carter just validated Byron's work. He helped Byron understand that he doesn't just go to church. He is the church.

Do you know what kind of relief that gives a burdened leader? Being a missionary in another country is exhausting. For sure. But what we in the church often forget is that it's the same for local missionaries. It's incredibly difficult to live into God's will for your life if you don't feel the support of your local church. It's even worse if you feel like they see you as a rebel or misfit. They see your outside efforts as a distraction. How backward is this theology?

Pastor Bryan's response was unusual because normally pastors are worried that if they encourage young people to continue serving in the city, they will serve even less in the church. But I have found the opposite to be true. If pastors value the work their congregants are doing, the congregants will naturally want to give value back to the church.

What I love about this story is that as Byron was sharing this with me, he told me about how he's now getting to use his fundraising experience to help lead a building campaign for the church. His gift was affirmed for the city and now it's being leveraged for the church.

2. HIGHLIGHT THEIR WORK

You know, every church has a John. Who is John? Well, John is the guy who is always at church whenever you need him. Early Sunday morning. Late Sunday afternoon. Wednesday night. Thursday night. Saturday morning. John is there. The church staff loves John. The pastor especially loves John. They tend to favor those who always volunteer at church.

Every church needs a John. They need John in spades. But I just want to point out one thing: not everyone can be John. And not everyone should be John. Because if John is always serving in the church, then he's never serving in the city.

We need people who do both. It's not either/or. It's both/and. Just make sure your church has a broad scorecard, or you might lose some of your most effective local missionaries. You'll definitely lose this next generation. I can't tell you how many great young leaders I've affirmed for their work—because their church hasn't—and they've broken down in tears when receiving affirmation. No one in spiritual authority has ever recognized their faithfulness. Who we choose to highlight reveals who we want our people to be. So keep filling the church walls with foreign missionary families and video testimonies with John on the parking team, but every now and then add the woman who started a nonprofit in the inner city or the business man you rarely see because he's making major moves for the kingdom. You might find some unlikely people perk up when they realize their work is considered sacred and valuable in your church. Especially business leaders who often can feel treated like ATMs but rarely are resourced for their wisdom and business savvy. We have a lot of room to grow in this area, but we also have a lot of potential for city impact when we do.

> Many great young leaders never get affirmed for their work, simply because it occurs outside the church.

3. COMMISSION THEM

When I graduated from high school, my church had a pretty big event for me and others going to Bible school for vocational ministry. One Sunday they brought us seniors before the congregation and commissioned us. My youth group had more than six hundred high school students, and we were being recognized in front of everyone! I felt pretty special, like people were counting on me. But now I wonder, "What were all my other friends thinking when they didn't receive the same commission? Surely God cared about their careers also?" I mean, the future chief of police could have been in that group. The next Chip and Joanna Gaines. The next president. Maybe even the researcher who cures cancer! But the only ones who got commissioned were those who felt called to work for a church. Does anyone else think this approach is a bit limited? I've always been under the impression that we were created in Christ Jesus for good works, even if it's in the marketplace.

We should commission people based not on what they do but rather on why they do it. What if we commissioned people who were willing to be Christ-loving, city-changing, church-investing, disciple-making local missionaries in their workplace? Once they've committed to the place and the people God has for them, we should consider them an extension of the church's mission in the city. I swear this would redeem Mondays. Christians, of all people, should not work for the weekends. But we do. According to Gallup's 2013 survey, almost no one enjoys their work. In the US, only 30 percent are "happy in their work," while 52 percent leave "feeling blah" after work and 18 percent "hate their jobs." That shouldn't be said of us. For Christians, Mondays should trigger mission, not misery. Even the worst bosses and the worst jobs have redemptive value because we are working unto the Lord.

4. CONNECT THEM

There's so much opportunity to convene leaders according to where they work. In our local missionary program, Initiative Network, we use the Seven Mountains as fields for mission.

- Business
- Arts
- Education
- Family
- Government
- Media
- Church

Where do you go if you want to be a Christian in politics? Where do you go if you want to view your work as worship? Where do you go if you want to meet other Christian educators in the school district?

We often group people in the church by their gender or age. But there are numerous benefits to grouping people by their work also. If you think about it, we don't choose our age, and we don't choose our gender, but we do choose our job. We labor over it, go to school for it, maybe even go into debt for it. Clearly we care about making a difference in a certain field. Then why not group people around their mission?

Imagine if we created space for teachers to connect with other teachers, entrepreneurs with other entrepreneurs, and artists with other artists. They're in our pews every week, but they spend the majority of their lives at work. So let's launch these local missionaries into our cities. The people in the pews may be the most untapped resource in the world. They want purpose. In Christ, they *have* purpose. We just need to connect and commission them. The gospel through the people of God could redeem every facet of our society.

Last thing. When you convene people, please, for love of the sweet King, don't *only* have pastors preaching to business leaders about business. It's about as patronizing as the young adult gatherings I go to where only married people preach to young singles about not stressing over getting married. That's easy for them to say. That's like a rich man convicting a poor man for even desiring money. So my advice is that you get various perspectives, but especially get leaders among the tribe to share.

5. UTILIZE THEIR STRENGTHS

Okay. So this is a big one. This is going to take some time for pastors to unlearn.

Imagine you meet four young people who are new to your church. Matt, who is an incredible videographer for a creative company. Stevi, who's one of the most gifted musicians and vocalists; she often plays at different venues all over the city. Monica, she's got drawing, painting, and design skills like no one's business. And then of course you've got Olivia, a prestigious wedding planner chick. All four just joined your church, and they want to serve.

Serve is a funny word to me in the church. Because it looks nothing like it did in the Bible.

I know pastors say, "Church is more than Sunday morning. Church is not a building. It's not an event!" Well, yeah, that sounds good, but why are nine out of ten serving opportunities in the building, at an event, on (drum roll) Sunday morning?

In the Acts church, it seemed like serving actually meant serving people outside the church.

Back to our videographer, musician, artist, and wedding planner friends wanting to serve. The average pastor sees those talents and thinks, *I've hit the jackpot.*

"Matt, can you help do video for us on Sunday?

"Stevi, can you help lead worship on Sunday?

"Monica, can you help do some design in our lobby, and maybe an art piece during worship on Sunday?

"Olivia, can you help us with event coordinating Sunday? Maybe even lead our volunteers?"

And they'll probably say yes.

But what if you took a different approach? What if you said, "Guys, I'm trying to move from doing ministry *to* millennials to doing ministry *through* millennials. We don't have many young adults here, so we need to go where they are. How about we do an event using all your talents in a place where you guys know a lot of young people already are?

"Matt, you can help promo the event with your video skills.

"Stevi, you and maybe some of your friends can do live music at it.

"Monica, you and some of your friends can design it aesthetically and add some creative elements to the night.

"Olivia, we've never done something like this before, so would you help coordinate the event, create an unforgettable night, like you do at all your weddings?

"We're going to give you budget for this, but it doesn't need to have our name on it. Our only request is that you give outsiders a place to belong and that you're strategic with gospel conversations."

Which approach do you think will light them up more?

Which one do you think will impact more people outside the church?

Really let that sink in.

And by the way, I don't think if you leverage them outside the church, that means they won't want to serve Sunday. I think you may find they want to be more involved. One, because you've leveraged their gifting like no pastor has before. Two, because they now need a place for the people reached that night to join. They need a community to plug them into. And luckily, that community is gathering next Sunday at your church.

> There's a huge difference between doing ministry *to* millennials and doing ministry *through* millennials.

MILLENNIALS are TIRED of HEARING ABOUT ACTS BUT NOT SEEING THEM

SEMINARY TRAINS PASTORS for the CHURCH

WE NEED TO TRAIN MISSIONARIES for the CITY

BUT...

For the Mom Who Just Doesn't Know What to Do

I get so many parents, but especially moms, approaching me for advice about their kids. Often, tears are quick to follow. These conversations are never easy.

The story is usually remarkably similar. They really love their kid, but things aren't going so great. Usually their son or daughter has walked away from the Lord, distanced themselves from the family, and possibly started to pursue things the parents know will only harm them.

There's a type of bond that happens when we go to the Lord to petition on behalf of someone else, especially when it's our own flesh and blood. So when we talk about them, we can quickly become emotional. I get it. For me, that's my youngest brother, Luke. After becoming a Christian, I prayed for him almost every day. I love this kid with all my heart. I've got such a soft spot for him and all his ridiculous antics. I think he's hilarious. I appreciate his originality. There's no one I've met like my brother Luke. He's infectious, and he's never met a stranger.

So it killed me when I saw him begin to throw his life away. Name it, and he's done it. Partying, alcohol, sex, drugs, drug dealing, drinking, getting robbed, getting stabbed, jail time, and rehab. There's no one I've prayed for more than Luke. But things weren't getting any better. In fact, they were getting worse. Way worse. Eventually Luke was so defiant and distant that there really was no way to speak into his life. It's not that he hated us, but he definitely was done with God. (He bought a tattoo kit and tattooed himself with a Hindu god on his arm in rebellion against the Christain God.)

I realized I was losing hope for his salvation. After ten years of trying, I was becoming numb in my prayers. Honestly, I was frustrated with God and tired of asking him for something I thought should have happened by now. Even worse, I didn't even have much time with Luke since he now lived with a girlfriend and rarely came around. Essentially, I had lost expectancy for my brother.

But something pricked my heart recently. A friend of mine, ChiChi, pointed out something about the woman in the Bible with the twelve-year blood issue. He talked about how she had every reason to give up hope, but she refused to. She wouldn't lose her expectation that God would change her circumstances, even after twelve years of pleading and no answer.

The woman fights through the crowd, certain that if she simply touches Jesus, she'll be healed. Well, she is right. After touching his robe, immediately she is healed. Jesus then asks who touched him. Incredulous, the disciples speak up and say, "You see the people crowding against you . . . and yet you can ask, 'Who touched me?'" (Mark 5:31).

The point being, "*Everyone* is touching you."

So everyone is touching Jesus, but only one person received healing from him.

But what's the difference between her and the others? She had expectation. I'd even say assumption. So it's possible to be in the presence of God and receive nothing because we expect nothing.

There's a saying about why you shouldn't assume. It makes something out of "u" and "me." But God, it seems like he loves when we assume. We tend to assume the worst. (That's where I was with Luke.) Like he's out to get us or he just doesn't care. But he has a pattern of showing up when we assume his goodness and his strength.

Just a couple of examples.

- Nowhere in the Bible does it say, "If you touch his cloak, you will be healed." She just assumed. She expected it.
- David told Goliath that he was going to cut his head off, and he didn't even bring a sword to the fight. That's a pretty big assumption. (God provided a sword. Goliath's sword.)
- One of my favorites is when the centurion stops Jesus from traveling to heal his servant. He says to just say the word and it'll be done. He didn't know that! He just assumed. He expected that kind of power. What was Jesus' response? After marveling at him and turning to the crowds, he said, "I tell you, I have not found such great faith even in Israel" (Luke 7:9).

So back to my brother Luke. I was ready to believe again. I quit assuming the worst of God's character, like he had forgotten me, and started assuming the best and expecting the best.

I remember praying, "God, I don't see Luke much anymore. We're not as close as we used to be. And he doesn't want anything to do with you. But I know you have children all across this earth. I pray you surround him with witnesses. Send messengers to him. I pray that you haunt him with good-news bearers. That he just can't avoid the gospel."

Well, a few weeks later, I got a call from Luke.

"Hey, Grant, I'm a waiter at this restaurant and there's a guy that seems really familiar who's become a regular. He's really cool. I swear he's one of those Christian singers Mom used to play on the radio all the time. What's the name of that guy that would always say 'GP, are you with me?' in his songs?"

"Kirk Franklin?!" I responded.

"Yes! That's the name! That's who it is. Is he pretty good?"

I said that he's not just known in the church but he's a nationally recognized and awarded musician. Suddenly he became nervous and excited over the phone and asked me, "What should I talk to him about?" My brother wants to be a musician, so it's like God gave me this answer in the moment. I said, "Ask him what he was doing when he was your age. Then ask him what he'd tell himself if he could go back to his old self." He replied, "Oh, that's good! Okay. I'm going to ask him." And he hung up.

Later that night, he texted me, "Woah. That guy just rocked my world."

Apparently during the conversation Kirk could sense my brother was going down the wrong path, so he grabbed his arm, looked him in the eye, and gave him some real talk and then some real encouragement. He said, "I can tell you're running from something and you're carrying it with you like a bag of luggage." It seems like that season became a turning point for my brother. Now many heart-to-hearts and God-stories later, my brother has started to pursue the Lord. And by the grace of God, he joined our 72 Program in Initiative, got some better community, plays in our band, and he's growing day by day.

▶ CHAPTER 13, "HEARING FROM LUKE"

I hope this story encourages you if you find yourself in a similar place with a loved one. I just asked God for a messenger. But he did me one better. He sent me Kirk Franklin! (Thanks, Kirk.)

I think God loves it when we assume the best of his power and character. Like a child who tells every kid in class, "My dad can beat up your dad." (I don't know why we do that. Sign our dads up for fights. But when we're young, we do.) Although I may not encourage him to say such things, if that were my son, I'd feel like a proud dad. I'd think, *My son truly believes I can do anything!* Let me tell you something, God truly can do anything. So if you're hitting the point where you feel like he doesn't care or maybe like he can't change your child, remember that he can take a heart of stone and replace it with a heart of flesh. And be confident that "the Lord is not slow in keeping his promise, as some understand slowness. Instead he is patient with you, not wanting anyone to perish, but everyone to come to repentance" (2 Peter 3:9).

Sometimes God is slower than our timing.

Sometimes he is faster than our timing.

But he is always better than our timing.

Just don't lose hope. Don't lose expectation. And never stop assuming that he's a good father who gives good gifts.

Stop Wearing a Mask to Church

We've all been there. Sunday morning. Mom wakes up. The kids are asleep. It's time for church. Well, it's time to get everyone ready for church.

I used to hope my mom would sleep through her alarm every Sunday. My brothers and I never wanted to go to church. *Mom, if God is everywhere, why do we have to go to church! Can't I worship him from my bed?* The best was when Mom was out of town on Sunday, because Dad usually didn't make us go. If he did, he took us to a different church that had donuts and lots of flat-screen TVs. We'd usually end up just staying in the lobby with the donuts and casually watching the service on one of the TVs. It was comfort over content, and my brothers and I liked that.

So as you can imagine, Mom was carrying the big burden of trying to lead our family every Sunday morning to a place none of us, besides her, really wanted to go.

But she never gave up. "Honey, are you going to help me or just sit there?" she would say to my dad. He would respond like most churchgoing men do. "Boys, do what your mom says."

We could tell by his lackluster reply that he didn't really want to go either, but since he didn't stand up to her, we were all trapped.

As a result, Sunday morning was chaotic. We had every excuse in the book not to go. We were sick. We had homework. We were atheists. None of it worked.

The car ride was somehow even worse. That's where the arguing usually broke out. By the time we pulled into the parking lot, Mom was not in the best of moods.

But here's how I knew the Holy Spirit was real. The second my mom crossed through the doorway of the church, she became a new creation. All of a sudden, her posture, her tone, her smile, all shined. It's as if the Spirit of the Lord struck her at that doorway and a heart of stone became a heart of flesh.

That, or she really cared about what people thought of her. I'll let you decide.

Don't we all care at some level?

But moms tend to really, really care. I've definitely had my fair share of the silent pinch in church so no one noticed I was acting up.

Here's the irony. The notion of church is come as you are, but often the ones who come the most come as they aren't.

Few places tempt us to wear a mask more than the church.

It wasn't just that the church doors transformed Mom. Jesus was in our home phone too. Well, at least if someone from the church came up on the caller ID. There could be anarchy in our home, but the moment she answered the phone, like an angel, she would say, "Hello. Oh, it's soooooo great to hear from you. How are you? Oh, things are great! We're doing really good." (But she never seemed to answer that way when bill collectors called.)

Sometimes it felt like *The Twilight Zone*.

This is important. Please hear me on this.

Discipleship is caught, not taught.

You may have taught your kids that Jesus loves them despite their flaws. But they may have caught, "*Only* if you act like you don't have flaws." The message being conveyed by these actions is this: "Kids, when you are around Christians, you have to be fake."

> We cannot afford to be fake in church.

The millennial generation is longing for something real. We cannot afford to be fake in church. We've all done it. It hasn't worked out for us.

This has to change.

Keep It Real

We must remember that Jesus said, "It is not the healthy who need a doctor, but the sick. I have not come to call the righteous, but sinners" (Mark 2:17). Millennials need to see and understand that Jesus really will bear our burdens, not simply judge us for having them.

When was the last time on a Sunday morning that someone asked you, "Hey, how are you?" and you replied, "Actually, not that good at all."

I remember going from event to event, traveling and speaking for a two-week stretch. I had just arrived at the convention center for a huge conference. It was one of the largest events I'd ever been invited to speak at. It was a high-energy environment, and I was up in one hour. There was only one problem.

I was exhausted. I was mentally, physically, and spiritually spent.

I was really worried because I tend to speak from the heart, which is great when my heart is healthy, but dangerous when my heart is running on fumes. It's very difficult for an empty cup to fill another cup. It's actually impossible. So I was going from tired and stressed to downright pleading with God to give me energy I just didn't have.

That's when this really bubbly lady who worked for the conference walked up to me. "Grant, we're so excited you're here! I can't wait for my kids to hear you speak! How are you feeling? Everything good?"

Moment of truth. Nothing in me wanted to be real with her. Sometimes it's hard for me to be real with bubbly people. And I didn't know her well. You know, just say, "Yeah, I'm good. I'm grateful to be here."

But the words of truth just started leaving my mouth. I think I was too mentally tired to play the game. The truth just slipped out.

"Actually, I'm so tired," I said. "I've been traveling a lot, speaking. With many late nights and many early flights. I'm a little worried because I was excited to speak at this event, but I've kind of hit a wall."

She quickly went from bubbly to concerned. "Grant, that totally makes sense. I can't imagine. How about this? There's a room I saw with a couch on the second floor of the convention center. It's pretty secluded. You can probably just lock the door and turn off the lights and take a quick nap, but set an alarm because you're up soon."

This lady must have been a prophet, because she had just spoken my love language: quality naps. Napping in obscure places is my spiritual gift. I'll nap in my car, in youth rooms, under boardroom tables, wherever. When I need sleep, I'll do whatever it takes. I have zero percent shame. Just give me twenty minutes, and I'm golden.

I thanked her profusely and then turned to go, but she asked to pray for me before I left. So she prayed over me. She did and it was like she flipped a switch. No joke. After she finished her prayer, I felt one hundred percent ready to go. Have you ever gone into prayer one way and come out another? That happened. I felt like a new man. But Lord knows, I still took that nap.

An hour later I stepped onstage, shared my heart, and it went great. Actually, it went better than I could have imagined. I remember leaving that night thinking, *Man, what if I hadn't been real with her earlier today? I would have gone on that stage trying to live off my own strength! Even if I could have fooled the crowd, I wouldn't have fooled God.*

I think in the same way, although we may not be on a stage, we sometimes wake up and go to church and try to *perform*. The irony is we've got nothing to give. David understood this when he said, "A broken and contrite heart you, God, will not despise" (Ps. 51:17).

> Sometimes we wake up, go to church, and try to *perform*.

Imagine if church lobbies were filled with people praying over one another's burdens rather than acting like we don't have them. What if we truly did become a house of prayer?

It wasn't until recently that I realized the nuance in the story of the paralyzed man whose friends lowered him through the roof. Matthew 9:2 says, "When Jesus saw their faith, he said to the man, 'Take heart, son; your sins are forgiven.'"

Jesus didn't just see the faith of the paralyzed man. He saw *their* faith. He saw the faith of his friends.

When we wear a mask, we hide our weaknesses, we live on fumes, and we forfeit the help we could receive when others bear our burdens. Sometimes we've lost hope, and we just need to borrow some of our friends'.

I know it's unlikely you'll walk into a church lobby filled with prayer, because the unspoken rule is that the longer you've been a Christian, the less you can hurt. Especially if you're in leadership. But this is outrageous because the more you give your life to God, the more you become a threat to the Enemy! So we, of all people, should be quick to share our faults.

I mean, let's just look at Paul. I would consider him closer to God than myself and anyone reading this book. I'd be happy just to get a glimpse of the second heaven, and this bro was invited to the third!

Yet still, knowing that God's power is perfected in weakness, Paul declares, "Therefore I will boast all the more gladly about my weaknesses, so that Christ's power may rest on me" (2 Cor. 12:9). He would *boast all the more gladly*. Not because he's proud of his weaknesses but because he's confident in God's response to them.

It's so unfortunate that receiving prayer is associated more with our weakness than with God's strength. The reality is there's no such thing as a strong Christian. Just weak Christians relying on a strong God.

PERFECTION IS A DISEASE, NOT A VIRTUE

Christians are not called to be perfect. We are called to chase perfection. This is what the righteous do; they seek God. But they aren't God. In seeking perfection, the righteous will inevitably fall.

All. The. Time. It's important that young people in the church understand this because legalism and hypocrisy are the byproducts of hiding failures. Proverbs 24:16 says that "the righteous fall seven times."

Not once.

Not twice.

Not three times.

Not four times.

Not five times.

Not six times.

The righteous fall seven times.

Remember, we're not talking about the wicked. We are talking about the people who are getting it right. They still fall, over and over again. But by God's grace, we don't stay in our failure. The verse in context says "though the righteous fall seven times, *they rise again*." We all fall. The Spirit just won't let us stay there. When we hide our moments of failure, we're also hiding our moments of grace.

One of the reasons I love the Bible so much is that it is full of people who love God but are deeply flawed and make huge mistakes. David. Solomon. Moses. Abraham. The disciples. Jonah. Pick a major figure of the Bible, other than Jesus, and you can find multiple examples of them sinning and making massive mistakes.

The righteous are made righteous by God's grace, which means we get to continue to pursue righteousness, even in our sin.

> Do our kids know they can fall and still be seen as righteous in the sight of God?

Do our kids know they can fall and still be seen as righteous in the sight of God? Do they know they can mess up big-time and still be welcome in the church? Do they know that being a Christian is not about being morally perfect and constantly having all the right answers?

Their understanding of God's grace depends on whether they

have been conditioned to run and hide when they sin, like Adam did, or to run *straight* to the Father when they sin, like David did. They can either cover themselves in shame or run to the Lord and say, "Search me, God, and know my heart" (Ps. 139:23).

When David messed up bad, he wrote these words to God.

> Have mercy on me, O God,
>   according to your unfailing love;
> according to your great compassion
>   blot out my transgressions.
> Wash away all my iniquity
>   and cleanse me from my sin.
>
> For I know my transgressions,
>   and my sin is always before me.
> Against you, you only, have I sinned
>   and done what is evil in your sight.
>
> —PSALM 51:1–4

David understood, on the deepest level, that he could always come to God, no matter how deep or awful his sin. It's crucial we get this, because we need God in order to please God. We're like a child needing to borrow money from their dad so they can buy him a present. Our hearts can't change for God unless they're changed *by* God. It's quite a paradox. The Man you're sinning against is the Man you're asking for help so you won't continue to sin against him.

And he's patient with us. He's so patient with us.

But Jesus goes even farther to make this point clear in the Gospels. He says that if someone sins against us, we should forgive them not just seven times but seventy times seven.

You know what the difference is between a righteous person and a sinner? One banks on forgiveness found in the cross, and the other doesn't. Christians are not better than anyone else. We're just forgiven. We didn't achieve salvation. We received grace.

So why are we constantly putting on a mask and acting like

we're perfect? It doesn't help us, and it definitely won't help the church reach the next generation. Millennials need real, not fake.

Being something you're not is exhausting. No one wins. You know the truth. God knows the truth. Your family probably also knows the truth. So why not just bank on his grace?

> Be confident in who you are, and comfortable with who you're not.

I know I'm young, but I've learned a big lesson in life: be confident in who you are, and comfortable with who you're not. We need more families like this. As believers, we've been freed from trying to keep up with the Joneses. It's hard enough to keep up with Jesus. Why exhaust ourselves trying to serve two masters?

▶ CHAPTER 13, "ROGER'S STORY: THE GIFT OF CEREBRAL PALSY"

EXPOSING OUR WEAKNESSES

I want to share a story of a family who invited someone into their lives, even though they knew it could get messy and their weaknesses would likely be exposed.

To be in our 72 Program (an eight-month learning community of seventy-two young leaders from forty different churches), you have to disciple someone. It's a requirement. One of the girls, Rachel, decided to disciple a girl at her church who looked up to her quite a bit. That girl's name was Audrey Chandler, the daughter of Matt and Lauren Chandler of the Village Church.

You probably know who Matt and Lauren are, but if not here's a little background. Matt and Lauren are a power couple for the kingdom. They're both writers and speakers, and Lauren is also a very gifted worship leader. The Village Church is one of the most popularly podcasted churches in the country, with millions of downloads over the last ten years, a shocking number of whom are very young listeners. I sometimes joke that Matt is like the pope to millennial Christians. They all listen to him.

So as you can imagine, you're in a pretty unique situation when you're discipling the daughter of the millennial pope. But that's not even the most unique part of the story.

Lauren Chandler was so thankful Rachel was pouring into her daughter because she wanted Audrey to have a young girl to look up to. Consequently, Lauren later felt led to prayerfully consider discipling Rachel. Through prayer, Lauren felt God telling her that "pouring into Rachel will have a natural overflow that will also pour into Audrey."

Lauren asked Rachel if she could disciple her, and of course, Rachel accepted. I mean, you're not really suffering for the gospel when Lauren Chandler asks to disciple you.

I think this was a brilliant response on Lauren's part. Parents are always discipling their children whether they like it or not. They live with you. They follow you. They pick up on things. So why not influence the one who influences your child?

The story would be cool if it ended right there. But it didn't. Soon after they started this discipleship journey, Lauren invited Rachel to come live with them!

This is why I'm telling this story. I often hear people describe not wanting to invite someone into their home life because they know that's when discipleship gets challenging. Once someone is in your home, they get to see the real you because they're always around. It's very hard to wear a mask around someone who lives in your home. It's even harder when you have a public platform and there are expectations you feel you have to live up to, what others expect your home life to look like.

The Chandlers knew that inviting someone into their home wasn't going to be easy.

Lauren told me, "When you invite someone in, it can get messy. Because we're not perfect and they're not perfect. So you've got to be willing to accept that it might not go the way you want it to. But that's okay, because God can do something in that."

To encourage the parents out there: Young people don't expect perfection, just honesty. One of Rachel's favorite things that the Chandlers did was simply sharing high-lows at the dinner table. Both Matt and Lauren were honest with their highs and lows of the day, and in turn so were their kids. This may seem simple, even too simple. But for my generation, having vulnerable conversations around the table is a dying art. I think parents would be surprised by what young people would learn from such talks, because to them it's nothing. But for us, it is everything.

> Young people don't expect perfection, just honesty.

Luckily for the Chandlers, it's not just messy for the one discipling. It's also messy for the disciple. It was encouraging to hear that Rachel isn't just getting free rent. She helps out a ton around the house. When I asked Rachel and Lauren what Rachel actually helps out with, they both started laughing. They mentioned how she often picks up the kids when they need rides. And apparently, she does a lot of sitting. As a young single, I didn't realize all the forms of sitting there are. Rachel helps with babysitting, house-sitting, dog-sitting, and even horse-sitting! Talk about a disciple being a blessing and not just a burden.

I asked Lauren what she would share with people who want to disciple but feel their lives aren't good enough to have someone follow them or join them. She said, "Ask the Lord, 'If we were to do this, show me who it would be.' And then trust God with his answer. Even if it gets messy. The messy parts of my family's life have probably spoken better to Rachel than the best parts that everyone else sees. Put yourself in that person's shoes. Wouldn't you want someone to embrace you at that age? Wouldn't you just be glad you got included? That you got to see that you're not the only one?"

As Lauren was saying this, Rachel nodded her head and said "yeah" a few times in agreement, almost like an amen. Rachel then added, "I think that Matt is an incredibly gifted and articulate pastor. I think Lauren leads with authority and passion. She's super gifted at leading worship. But when I think of them, I don't really think of those things. I think of them as a husband and wife, as a father and mother. Of course, they have shaped me as my pastors, but more so as a family."

This is huge! We often are nervous to invite someone into our mess because they will see we aren't as godly as we seem. Inviting someone in also invites a whole other level of accountability.

Some of us think we're not gifted enough to disciple. We haven't been trained. We're not well read. We don't have a leadership bone in our body. But I love this story because Rachel got time with a couple whose influence is exponential, but she didn't see them for their platform. She saw them as parents. She didn't see them for their ministry. She saw them for their marriage.

It makes me think maybe we're making discipleship harder than it needs to be.

You may not have a big platform, but you may be a good parent.

You may not have a huge ministry, but you may have a healthy marriage.

Real faith is messy. It requires vulnerability. It requires trust. But it's worth every second. Real faith doesn't require you to be a pastor. It just requires that you're obedient with whoever God has put before you.

Dietrich Bonhoeffer said, "One act of obedience is better than one hundred sermons."

What is one small thing God is calling you to be obedient in today? Start there.

SOMETIMES WE WAKE UP, GO TO CHURCH, AND TRY TO "Perform."

BE CONFIDENT IN WHO YOU ARE & comfortable WITH WHO YOU'RE NOT

CHAPTER 14

FATHERS, BE GOOD
TO YOUR FAMILIES

I don't know what you were doing in 1990, but two things happened that year that really impacted my life. First, I was born
in January, so that was a pretty big deal for me. Second, one of the
best shows ever, *The Fresh Prince of Bel-Air*, debuted in September
of 1990. If you don't know, this is the show that launched Will
Smith's career to a whole new level. It's definitely one of the most
memorable shows of the '90s. It doesn't hurt that it also has the
most quotable intro song of all time.

On IMDB, the highest-rated episode contains what is considered the most powerful moment in the show's six-year run of 148
episodes. It was raw, real, and close to home for any young person
who's felt neglect from their father. In reference to James Brown's
song "Papa's Got a Brand New Bag," they titled the episode "Papa's
Got a Brand New Excuse." In the episode, Lou Smith, Will's father,
abruptly shows up after fourteen years of abandoning him. He's a
truck driver now and said he was just passing through. Although
Will suddenly turns into a giddy child, ready to pick up with his
dad like nothing ever happened, Uncle Phil is concerned Lou is
going to let Will down once again.

Unfortunately, Uncle Phil is right. Moments before Will and
Lou are supposed to leave for a summer trip in his dad's truck, Will

puts down his bags to receive the news that something else has come up and they have to postpone the trip.

It's clear the trip is never going to happen. As his father walks out of Will's life for the last time, Will tries to be strong and shrugs it off like it doesn't matter to him. But it's obvious he's suppressing his true feelings.

Here is the script from the scene.

UNCLE PHIL: Will, it's all right to be angry.

WILL: Hey, why should I be mad? At least he said goodbye this time. I just wish I hadn't wasted my money buying this stupid present.

Will pulls out a small African-style statue of a father sitting with his son on his lap.

UNCLE PHIL: I'm sorry. If there was something that I could . . .

WILL: You know what, you ain't got to do nothing, Uncle Phil. It ain't like I'm still five years old. Ain't like I'll be sitting up every night asking my mom, "When's Daddy coming home?" Who needs him? He wasn't there to teach me how to shoot my first basket, but I learned and got pretty good at it too.

UNCLE PHIL: Yeah. You did!

WILL: Got through my first date without him. I learned how to drive, I learned how to shave, how to fight. I had fourteen great birthdays without him. He never even sent me a damn card.

Will turns and shouts toward the door his father walked through.

WILL: To hell with him! I didn't need him then and I don't need him now. You know what, Uncle Phil? I'm gonna get through college without him. I'll get a great job without him. I'll marry a beautiful honey, have a bunch of kids, and be a better father than he ever was. I don't need him for that, because there ain't a damn thing he could ever teach me about how to love my kids.

After a long pause . . .

Will: How come he don't want me, man?

Will breaks down crying, and Uncle Phil comforts him. The episode ends with a close-up of the statue that Will bought for his father.

▶ Chapter 14, "Will's Father Leaves Once and for All"

This scene was filmed in only one shot. If you YouTube the scene, you'll notice that Will's hat becomes a hindrance when they hug. They'd normally shoot the scene again, but the makers of the show knew *that* was the scene meant for the show. It caught everyone off guard because Will was supposed to just shrug off his father for abandoning him, but Will ad-libbed what he felt like so many youth have to go through when their father neglects them. Everyone on the set was in tears.

It's no secret that we have a problem with masculinity in America. We don't even know what healthy masculinity is. Is it a really tough guy who drives a big truck? A successful businessman who lives in a big house? Is it a sensitive soul who is in touch with his feelings? What does it mean to be a real man? What does it mean to be a good father?

I'm not sure I know that answer. All I know is that my generation has been impacted greatly by the confusion over fatherhood, and the church hasn't done a lot to address the problem. Which is why millennials remind me of the crowds Matthew describes: "When [Jesus] saw the crowds, he had compassion on them, because they were harassed and helpless, like sheep without a shepherd" (Matt. 9:36).

Millennials today are harassed and helpless sheep without a

shepherd. They are trying to do what is right in their own eyes, and it's not working out for them. They're the most fatherless generation we've seen in the history of our nation. So any church that wants to reach out to millennials is going to need to teach, model, and embody what it means to be a faithful father. Our response shouldn't be cynicism. Our response should be compassion.

> Millennials are harassed and helpless sheep without a shepherd.

Forms of Fatherhood

Now, when I talk about my generation being fatherless, I don't just mean kids who are raised by single moms. Fatherlessness is more complicated than that. Check out the chart "Forms of Fatherhood."

DEADBEAT DAD

I know this is a harsh title, but it's the only one in my list I didn't come up with. This is what our culture calls men who bail out on their responsibility to their family. It is harsh but I think it's appropriate. If a man has become a father, he has a duty to then *be* a father. A deadbeat dad is a dad who refuses to be a father and is either totally absent from his child's life or exists somewhere on the periphery.

DISTANT DAD

This is the dad who plagues the church. The dad who is there but not really there. This is the dad who shows up at the game but keeps his head buried in his phone the entire time. The dad who comes to church but only because his wife forced him to. This is the most common dad of my generation, and perhaps the one who has done the most damage in the church. The major sin of the church is that we have allowed this dad to run rampant.

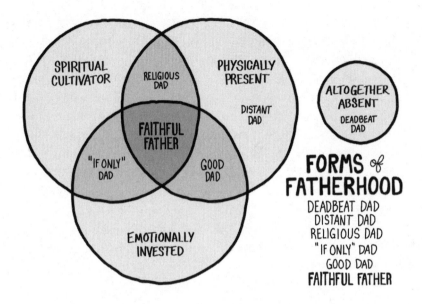

Deadbeat dads see their kids as burdens as opposed to blessings, which is why they leave. A distant dad, however, doesn't leave physically. Instead he sticks around but leaves spiritually and emotionally. He is with his child physically, but his mind is still back at the office.

Often this dad gives the majority of his energy to endeavors outside the home and gives what is left over to his family.

Here is the difference between a deadbeat dad and a distant dad. The child of a deadbeat dad can say, "My dad chose to leave my mother and me when I was young. At this point, I don't really remember him."

The child of a distant dad can say, "My dad didn't choose to leave my mother and me when I was young. But he does choose to leave us every night when he comes home from work. At this point, I don't really know him."

> A distant dad is physically present but emotionally distant and spiritually absent.

A deadbeat dad leaves one day. A distant dad leaves every day.

He is physically present but emotionally distant and spiritually absent. The craziest thing about this kind of dad is I've seen him in leadership in the church—a lot. He might be a deacon or an elder. Perhaps even a pastor. He is well respected in the church, but his family knows the truth about him. They know he prioritizes the needs of others over the needs of his own family. My heart really hurts for the faithful women who continue to support and pray for these men. The Bible clearly says men are supposed to be the spiritual leaders of the home. But this kind of dad settles for simply providing financially for the family and then leaves the spiritual and emotional needs to the mom.

This kind of dad is stuck. He's lost his kids because they don't really know him. Instead of being a transformational leader in the home, he is simply a transactional ATM for his family, necessary in times of need but absent for the rest of life.

RELIGIOUS DAD

This dad wants the family in church, but he never communicates why it's important. You might say he is religious but not spiritual. For this dad, being in church is more about doing the "right thing" than about making sure his family cultivates a healthy relationship with the Lord. Because there's a lack of emotional connection, this dad can make God seem like a taskmaster. Even a killjoy. Rules without a relationship breeds rebellion. This form of parenting can make kids bitter toward God and especially toward the church.

"IF ONLY" DAD

This is the dad I fear I could one day become. Gulp.

This dad puts in the hard work of emotionally investing in his children. This dad puts in the hard work of developing a spiritual relationship with his kids. This dad totally gets that he needs to be the spiritual leader of his home. The problem is that this dad also wants to be this for lots of other people, and he is not home enough to experience the benefits of his labor. He is a terrific role model for his kids, but he's too often being this from too great a distance.

He's just not home enough. It's not that he's out drinking with his buddies or playing golf. He is doing good things in the world, but that doesn't change the fact that he's gone. Gone is gone.

His kids would say, "I love my dad. I wouldn't be who I am today without him. But I wish he had been around more. If only he had been around more."

I travel a lot for speaking engagements. There are many weeks when I barely sleep in my own bed. It's not a big deal now because I'm single without any kids. But there are nights I wonder what this would be like if I had a family. It would be hard. Of course, I have my thoughts about taking my family with me and dating my wife in different cities and exposing my children to as many different cultures as possible, but I also know there is the reality of needing to provide children a stable and consistent home life. I know a lot of men must be road warriors to provide for their families, and I imagine the traveling causes great stress in the home.

The "if only" dad has the right intentions. He wants to do right by his family and the world. His problem is one of priority.

I think the greatest downside and my greatest fear is that my ministry could be a stumbling block to my children's relationship with God. None of the "if only" dads would ever want that, but that's the real danger. There is nothing wrong with wanting to go out in the world and do great things for the gospel, but it should never be done at the expense of your family.

GOOD DAD

This dad may go to church every Sunday. He may have fun with his kids on the weekend, taking them to soccer games and the lake for fishing or whatever. But he is not the spiritual leader in his home. He is not a spiritual cultivator.

He provides for his kids, but he isn't providing what they truly need: spiritual direction. For whatever reason, these men treat God like he's in the mothering category. They often defer to Mom for spiritual things. I've heard so many young girls say, "My dad is a great guy. I have so many great memories with my dad. But Dad didn't really talk to me about God much. He usually left that up to Mom."

The interesting thing about this guy is he can be found intimidating his daughter's new date, but he can't be found instigating his daughter's new faith. He can play the macho part but not the part that requires spiritual vulnerability.

I remember Matt Chandler highlighting this phenomenon to a group of young women: "Can I say something to young ladies here? I'm trying to pick my words carefully here. Your husband, whoever he is, single ladies, will have an unbelievable amount of influence over your sons and daughters in regards to spiritual things. If you want your children to love Jesus deeply, hold out for a man that is godly. And let me tell you this: I am well aware that godly men are rare. Lots of neat Christian boys, not a lot of godly men. And we're working our tails off to try to develop some into that. But don't settle, because it's better that you be lonely now than you be married and lonely later. Are you tracking with me? It is better that you be lonely now than for you to get married to a man who will teach your kids everything but the way of Jesus."

> "Godly men are rare. Lots of neat Christian boys, not a lot of godly men."
>
> **—MATT CHANDLER**

Now, don't get me wrong. These men have fun. These men prioritize their family. These men make many memories and many moments that are to be applauded. They just haven't prioritized the faith of their family as a personal responsibility. I think deep down you'd find that there's a desire to be a spiritual leader, but maybe they missed it. Maybe they just don't know what it looks like. But at the end of the day, they are active, good dads, but they are passive spiritual fathers.

FAITHFUL FATHER

I've found God to be unpredictable in his methods. He's always on the move, always shaking things up in our lives. Sometimes it's hard to know what exactly he's even up to. But one thing is for sure.

God wants our hearts.

That's what he is after. He searches our hearts. He guards our hearts. He even delights in us when our hearts are broken and honest before him. He wants to transform every crevice and every corner of our hearts, and I think that's at the core of what a faithful father does.

A faithful father is still dating his wife. It could be years after marriage, but he's still pursuing her heart. The same goes for his kids. Even though his kids have grown up and are now sometimes embarrassed to be around him, he won't give up on them. He's finding new ways, new tactics. A faithful father realizes his kids are daily waking up to a battle for the allegiance and alliance of their hearts. So the faithful father doesn't just ask, "How was your day?" He wants to know, "How is your heart?" He's grounded in God's Word. He asks for forgiveness often. And he strives to never settle for giving leftover energy to his wife and kids after work.

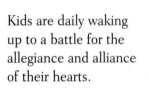

Kids are daily waking up to a battle for the allegiance and alliance of their hearts.

He's patient yet relentless, just like our Father in heaven.

God doesn't just focus on the surface-level stuff. He is willing to do the tedious, surgical scalpeling to heal our hearts. It reminds me of how C. S. Lewis explains our relationship with God: "Imagine yourself as a living house. God comes in to rebuild that house. At first, perhaps, you can understand what he is doing. He is getting the drains right and stopping the leaks in the roof; you knew those jobs needed doing, so you are not surprised. But presently he starts knocking the house about in a way that hurts abominably and doesn't seem to make any sense. What on earth is he up to? The explanation is that he is building quite a different house from the one you thought of—throwing out a new wing here, putting on an extra floor there, running up towers, making courtyards. You thought you were being made into a decent little cottage: but he is building a palace. He intends to come and live in it himself."[17]

Since the main goal of life is to love God with all your heart, soul, and mind, this dad has made this the highest priority for the hearts, souls, and minds of his children. He wants them to have life, and life to the fullest.

I remember reading a study by Focus on the Family that showed what happened when different members of unchurched families came to Christ.

The study revealed that when a father comes to Christ, there is a 72 percent chance that his wife and children will eventually give their lives to the Lord also. But you know what happens if the mother comes to Christ? There is only a 16 percent chance the husband and children will follow suit. And when a child comes to Christ, there is just a 6 percent chance that the parents and siblings will join in.

When a man vulnerably walks with the Lord, God puts a type of influence on him that impacts everyone around him. I'm scared that we Christian men might be missing it, even neglecting it, because we're hoping the church or our wives will influence our families for us.

"I'll make him a man; you make him a Christian" is how the thinking often goes. It may be normal, but it isn't biblical.

In the end, it all comes down to Jesus. I'm not saying faithful fathers are perfect. And I'm definitely not saying good dads aren't Christians. I'm saying that for a faithful father, Jesus doesn't just describe him. Jesus defines him.

So what if we looked to Jesus as our role model for manhood?

He was humble, he was strong, and he sacrificed everything. Jesus was marked by an unconventional, unconditional, unbelievable love this world had never seen before.

> A man's ability to lead his family is completely dependent on his ability to follow Jesus.

If we have a skewed image of what it means to be a man, it affects everything: our family, our friends, our future, our legacy. A man's ability to lead his family is completely dependent on his ability to follow Jesus. So women shouldn't be looking for a man who will meet all their needs. They should be looking for the man who will send them to the God who can.

For the Dad Who Wants to Change

Let me acknowledge something. If you're a dad reading this and you feel like you've fallen short of being the father you always thought you'd be, there's hope for you. Lots and lots of hope. Yes, trying to change now, after years of neglect, may feel like the most uncomfortable thing you've ever been asked to do.

I want to encourage you.

First, there's a pretty good chance your dad wasn't the ideal model of a man for your family either. This fatherless problem goes back really far and hits really deep in the heart of men. But the buck can stop here. For that to happen, you need to have a hard conversation with your wife and kids that will probably involve confession, repentance, and a plan of action.

It's never easy to have hard conversations, especially with the people you love. It may seem long overdue. It may even seem too late. But it's not.

A Chinese proverb says, "The best time to plant a tree was twenty years ago. The second-best time is now."

But can I share something with you?

Whatever you're about to tell your kids, they probably already know.

What they don't know is that you want to change.

Not that you *have* changed.

But the Spirit of God has convicted you to the point of desiring change. You're ready to take a new journey, and you're willing to put things in place to make it happen.

I want to share an encouraging story from my friend Mitch Tidwell and his father. Listen to his testimony.

> When I was growing up, my dad was an awful father. He was verbally abusive to everyone in the family. We were always walking

on eggshells around him. I grew up feeling like I couldn't do anything right.

I hated my dad. I hated his guts. My mom and dad were going to get a divorce, and I was happy about it. Everyone in our family was happy about it, because he was that bad of a father.

When my dad came to Christ, that was a big moment in our lives—a Holy Spirit moment. I remember him saying to me, "Hey, I can't change what I did, but I can change how I go forward."

And I get emotional even thinking about it now, because from that moment on, in his own imperfect and humble way, he started to love my mom so well.

I could forgive him, because I saw his repentance. It has made such a tremendous difference on my family, and on my life. I think the very best thing any dad could do for their kids is love their mom very, very well.

My dad is a truck driver, not a counselor, but I know of at least four different men he's ministered to in their broken marriages. Most of the marriages were coming to the end of their rope. And as of today, three of the four marriages are still together and even stronger than before; two of those men came to Christ in the process.

It's never too late.

I've found it to be really hard to criticize a man genuinely asking for forgiveness. Most young adults would tear up just to see their dad acknowledge his shortcomings and their impact on the family.

> How we see our father impacts how we see the Father.

For people my age, just seeing our dad initiate the conversation would open up the floodgates of healing. It's not easy, but it is necessary.

We have to remember, how we see our father impacts how we see the Father. So when our fathers are transformed, so is the church—and so is this generation.

A MAN'S ABILITY TO **LEAD** **HIS FAMILY** IS COMPLETELY DEPENDENT ON HIS ABILITY TO **FOLLOW** JESUS.

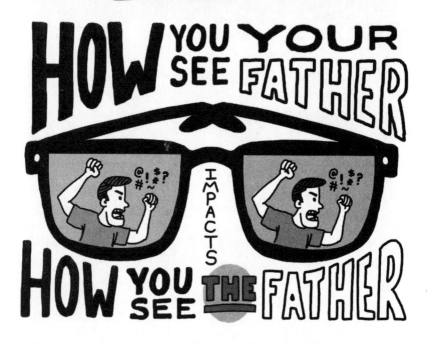

CHAPTER 15

FEARFUL, EXCITING
OBEDIENCE

When I was in elementary school, I was told I needed to learn cursive. Which was awesome, except for the fact that I hated cursive. "That's grown-up writing," I would say. It was very meticulous and difficult to pick up. I mean, we had just learned to write normal sentences. And now we had to use these elegant squiggly lines to write too! What does a second grader need cursive for? It was tough, but we all pushed on and learned the new writing technique because, even though we weren't going to use cursive as kids, we believed what our teacher was telling us. Mrs. Raby would insist, "Knowing cursive is going to be very important when you grow up!"

Well, Mrs. Raby lied.

I'm now twenty-seven, and cursive is as relevant to me as my old Myspace account. Maybe when I turn thirty, I'm going to be bombarded by cursive-dependent obligations. But I really don't think so. These days, you don't need to know how to write in cursive at all. No one even checks your signature when you sign for something. I often sign with a smiley face because I just want someone to check.

I'll give it to Mrs. Raby. There was no way she could have known our society was going to change like this. Cursive had

always been important, so everyone assumed it would be important in the future.

So follow me on this one. I liken evangelism in the church to cursive. When you're in the youth group, you're constantly told things like this:

"Be on fire for Christ!"
"Invite all your friends to church!"
"Tell everyone you know about Jesus!"
"Change your school with the gospel!"
"Make him known, on and off the field!"
"Be a city on a hill, set apart from the other kids at school!"

In youth group, you are saturated with the Great Commission. Then you grow up, go to "big church," and learn this disturbing reality: very few people live this way. You'll be hard-pressed to find people in the pews who are sharing the gospel with their neighbors (if they even know them), who are changing their workplace for Christ, and who are using their talents to impact the city.

It seems that the older we get, the safer we live. But safe faith isn't compelling to young adults. (I don't know if it's even biblical.)

I often get asked, "Why has the younger generation abandoned the church?" My immediate thought is, *Why has the older generation abandoned the mission?*

> The older we get, the safer we live. But safe faith isn't compelling to young adults.

A recent study by LifeWay Research found that 70 percent of young adults leave the church at the age of nineteen. So if you help on Wednesday nights, you can count on more than half of those kids to walk away in the near future. They even found that "80 percent of young people who dropped out of church said they did not plan to do so during high school."[18] Something is triggering this unparalleled evacuation.

Ironically, in an article titled "Is Evangelism Going out of Style?" the Barna Group reported that "the practice of evangelism has either remained the same or declined among different generations of born-again Christians, except for one. For millennials the practice of evangelism is notably on the rise,"[19] with a 9 percent increase.

If you think about these two studies, they're basically saying there is a mass exodus of young people from the church, but they're sharing their faith once they're out. It's as if they're graduating from the church but not necessarily abandoning the faith. It seems that this younger generation sees the need for this dark world to know Christ but doesn't see the church as a viable way to make that happen.

It's a lot safer to just be a believer and not be a disciple maker. Then you can agree but not do. There's less risk involved when we just agree with Jesus. We abandon the mission because it costs us too much—our time, our resources, and especially our convenience.

Have you ever noticed that older people don't usually have scabs? Think about it. Scabs are what you get when you're young. You get them on the playground from running too fast, jumping too high, or playing too hard. But as you get older, you don't attempt anything that could give you scabs. Because our bodies have more to lose if something goes wrong.

Again, the older you get, the safer you live. It seems this is true of our faith journey also. Have we restricted the glory days of our faith to our youth?

I remember hearing Francis Chan talk about his frustration with this notion. Both of his parents passed away in their for-ties, so it taught him to number his days. He talked about how he never knows if this is his last day before meeting Jesus. But instead of letting this sobering reality paralyze him, he's allowed it to ignite his faith. He said, "It just doesn't make sense to me. If you're that close to seeing God, why are we living such a safe life? And what the heck are we saving for? We go backward in the church, where we do crazy things when we're eighteen, and then we start to live safer and safer every year."

> Have we restricted the glory days of our faith to our youth?

You know, I once had a roommate who got me hooked on the popular show *The Walking Dead*. We would watch it almost every week. It was the kind of show where you could get really attached to a character, and then one false move, boom—they're dead. I was hooked. There was only one problem. It was season 5 that I was watching with him. So when the season was over, I still needed to catch up.

I went back to the first season and found there were some other really great characters I got attached to. But I always knew who was going to die. No matter how much screen time a character got, I knew, "If they ain't in five, they ain't alive."

It sort of added more suspense to the question of which charac-ters I loved were going to die. I'd watch, thinking, *Death is coming for you, man. I know it! Is today the day?* But on the flip side, it also took away a ton of fear for my favorite characters who I knew would make it. No matter how close they got to death, I wasn't worried. I was actually more invested, wondering, *How in the world are they going to get out of this one?* Something always worked out, right in the nick of time, and they made it out alive.

It made me think. Shouldn't Christians live with this type of confidence? Don't we know how it's going to end? Why aren't we living like we're going to make it? We're all going to be alive after five!

Consider this: if today truly were your last day, what would you do with it?

I can guarantee that whatever you'd do, it wouldn't be safe. It would involve meaningful risk. Whether it was restoring a broken relationship, telling that loved one about Jesus, or fulfilling an item on your bucket list. It wouldn't be safe.

Let's talk about the disconnect, and what kind of leaders young people are looking for in the church.

There's a guy I love telling older generations to look into, because he does live like we're going to make it. There's an idea that you have to dress really cool, be up to date with pop culture, use all the new slang, maybe get some tattoos, and then maybe you'll be able to connect with young people for Jesus. But there's a guy named Bob Goff who is breaking all the rules. He's just being unashamedly, unapologetically who God's called him to be, and it's a breath of fresh air for young people.

A few years ago, some friends and I had the privilege of grabbing lunch with Bob. And by that I mean he put his phone number in the back of his national bestselling book, so I called him. (Talk about making yourself available for people to join your life.) It was one of the coolest experiences because Bob told me something I'm never going to forget. Let me preface it, however, by saying Bob is a husband, father, bestselling author, public speaker, the director of Restore International, a lawyer, a professor, and the honorary consul of the Republic of Uganda. He's also fifty-eight years old.

244 ■ Part 2: What Millennials Look For in Church

Baffled by the amount of work he does for the kingdom, I asked, "Bob, how are you able to do so much? It's inspiring. But honestly, I don't know how you get it all done at your age."

"I don't sleep," he told me without missing a beat. My friends and I laughed because we thought he was joking. He continued, "No. Really. I don't sleep. Last night I slept for five hours and got my first call from Uganda at five in the morning." He smiled and then said three sentences I will never forget. "I want to die exhausted. We have eternity to rest. Until then, let's do things."

> When Christians have outlandish, outrageous faith, it reveals cultural Christianity for what it actually is: boring and ineffective.

That statement was so incredibly simple yet so incredibly profound. It wasn't inspiring because Bob works so hard and doesn't sleep. It was inspiring because he's a fifty-eight-year-old man who dares to sacrifice his sleep and comfort for a greater cause. I have never in my life heard an older Christian say anything remotely close to "I want to die exhausted" for the gospel's sake. A statement like that is seen as irresponsible and audacious. But I think the church needs to redeem the word audacity. Sometimes what the world calls audacity, God calls childlike faith.

When Christians have outlandish, outrageous faith, it reveals cultural Christianity for what it actually is: boring and ineffective. That kind of faith is contagious. And when it's coming from an older Christian, it's inspiring. It makes young people think, *Man, I want to have that kind of faith at that age. What will it take for me to live like that when I'm older?*

Steven Furtick said, "If the size of the vision you have for your life isn't intimidating to you, there's a good chance it's insulting to God." And just to be clear, a big vision doesn't need to be moving to another country or having a large platform. It just has to involve doing something that scares you a bit, but excites you a ton. My generation wants to be discipled by older men and women who walk in a little fear and excitement when they respond to the Lord.

When you think about it, there's no story in the Bible without a little fear and excitement. God always calls us into the unknown.

I've never seen one single story in the Bible where God enters someone's life and says, "You know what? You're doing great. Just keep doing what you're doing."

No. He always calls his people to a new level of obedience, if not a new direction entirely. God enters Paul's life, and everything changes. God

> I've never seen one single story in the Bible where God enters someone's life and says, "Just keep doing what you're doing."

enters Jonah's life, and everything changes. God enters David's life, Moses' life, Mary's life. The list goes on and on. He's a disruptive God. Even Job, who actually was doing great, had his life changed when God intervened. No one is safe.

I think Jacob got to do physically what we get to do daily, and that is wrestle with God.

In 2005, Steve Jobs gave a commencement speech at Stanford. He shared with the students a profound practice that he did daily. Every day, Steve Jobs looked in the mirror and asked himself the question, "If today were the last day of your life, would you want to be doing what you're doing?" He then observed, "Whenever the answer has been no for too many days in a row, I know I need to change something."[20]

I'd say, whenever the answer has been no for too many days in a row, you're probably not hearing God's voice. Or you're not responding to his leading. Because he isn't silent. He's quite loud once you want to hear. I just don't know if we want to hear him. I think this is why Jesus often said, "Whoever has ears, let them hear." Of course everyone has ears, but only a few use them.

Have you ever heard the Holy Spirit referred to as the Comforter? That's such a funny name to give the Holy Spirit. Talk about misleading! Sometimes I think that name is just an inside joke they giggle at in heaven, because here's the truth. In all my life, no one has asked me to do more uncomfortable things than the Holy Spirit!

He's always got something new for me to do, and it's rarely safe, easy, or convenient.

However, over the years, the Holy Spirit's direction has become less scary and more exciting. Not because there's no risk now. If anything, the stakes are higher. The difference is that I've seen his faithfulness. I've even seen his ridiculousness. I've seen him show up, and I've seen him show off.

> Show me a church led by fearful, exciting obedience, and I'll show you a church full of young people forming new heroes.

I feel like God is slowly but surely trying to make us comfortable in the uncomfortable. Our plans and God's plans don't always line up. But maturity comes when we trust his ways more than our wants.

When was the last time you felt God calling you to do something that scared you but also got you a little excited to see how your obedience could play out?

This generation will continue abandoning the church if the church continues to abandon the mission. But show me a church led by fearful, exciting obedience, and I'll show you a church full of young people forming new heroes.

Watching God Show Up

When I was twenty years old, God called me into fearful, exciting obedience. My friend Jon Pendergrass had started a nonprofit and asked me to be one of the guys to help him lead it. Jon had a great vision, so I went for it, even though I was totally out of my comfort zone. Jon's idea was to help local churches do local mission projects that were within ten minutes of their location. We were trying to give churches opportunities to love their actual neighbors. We'd be right in the middle of things, working with the city and the neighborhood to inquire about needs and then getting the church plugged in to be the hands and feet of Christ. It was hard work, but it was super fun. Every week presented us with new problems, which meant every week we got to see God show up in new ways.

> Every week presented us with new problems, so every week we got to see God show up in new ways.

We never felt like we had what we needed to get the job done. We didn't have the money or the experience or the credibility or the connections. All we had was the confidence that God called us to go and do this work. So we banked on that confidence and leaned hard into Jesus.

One day we were revving up for our largest mission project to date with the youth group from the Village Church. The plan was to gather enough service projects for their five hundred students to do a day of service in the Lewisville community. Believe it or not, knocking on strangers' doors and asking if you can serve them, even when their yard or house looks like it needs a lot of serving, isn't easy. "Who are you?" was a pretty common reaction. Sometimes the tone wasn't too pleasant. People have a really hard time receiving free help. That's why you need someone as the middleman, a person of peace who has trust among the community. By the grace of God, the city connected us to a local guy named Alvin Turner, and he happened to be a believer. Once Alvin trusted us, he gave us the golden ticket. He looked us straight in the eyes and said, "When you knock on doors in this neighborhood, just tell them you come in my name." (At first I was little skeptical. Who is this guy? And who the heck even talks like that? *Good people, we come to you in the name of Sir Alvin Turner.*) Alvin had lived in the neighborhood his whole life. He had invested most of it loving his neighbors, and he had the trust to prove it. He was the first man I ever met whom I'd consider to be a true local missionary.

So we told people we came in Alvin's name, and that made all the difference.

As soon as people heard we were friends with Alvin, we got invited in for sweet tea, for dinner, and for more conversation. Since we came in Alvin's name, they were willing and eager to know our names.

Alvin had served this neighborhood faithfully, and the people loved him for it. We ended up with dozens of homes and families for us to serve. We had never seen God show up as much as he did on this event.

But then we ran into a little problem. Actually, it was a huge problem, and it happened just three days before the big day.

Our team was meeting at Starbucks, and we realized that we had more than five hundred kids coming to serve but no way to get them to the event. We *thought* we had thought of everything. We had the community to serve. We had city hall donating resources. And we had hundreds and hundreds of volunteers. But we had no buses. My team wrongly assumed that the pastors worked out transportation. And the pastors wrongly assumed we did. Oops.

The panic and scrambling began. Idea after idea started coming out as we considered every option and exhausted every idea. After about an hour of coming up with solutions, we landed on just trying to recruit as many volunteer drivers from the Village as we could. We needed ninety drivers, to be exact. In three days. We knew it would be really tough to find that many drivers, and we now needed a new waiver for their parents to sign. So it basically was going to be a logistical nightmare! But what choice did we have? The event was in three days.

As our meeting was coming to a close, a man sitting next to us suddenly pulled off his headphones and said, "Hey, can I say something to you guys?" We all were curious why he'd interrupt us, since he'd been listening to music while working on his computer the whole time. But the man continued, "So I'm going to be honest. I was kind of eavesdropping, and I heard you guys talking about what you're doing in Lewisville." He went on to explain that he just moved to town two weeks ago. "And you're not going to believe this," he said, "but I moved here because I just bought a charter bus company." What in the world! He then went on to say, "I'd love to help you guys with your project this weekend. How many buses do you need, and when do you need them? I got it covered."

Immediately, Blake, the most sarcastic pastor in our group, patted my back and shouted with a smile, "See, Grant, I told you God has cattle on a thousand hills!"

Everyone burst into laughter. (Being a new Christian, I had no idea what that meant.)

But then it got even better.

The man asked for the address to send his bus drivers to Saturday. We told him the address, and he said, "Wait a minute. Is that the Village Church?"

We told him it was, curious as to why he was asking.

Now he was the one laughing. "God is funny. My wife just dragged me to that church last Sunday morning."

> Sometimes God likes to show up. And sometimes he likes to show off.

Sometimes God likes to show up. And sometimes he likes to show off.

But he can't show off if we play it safe.

Does your church give God a reason to show up?

Obedience is our job. Outcomes are his.

But too often we're scared to take a step forward, because we don't feel adequate. This is God's playground—flipping our inadequacies into testimonies. One moment we had no transportation and no good ideas, the next we had charter buses with reclining seats and a movie for the road.

Francis Chan said, "I don't want my life to be explainable without the Holy Spirit. I want people to look at my life and know that I couldn't be doing this by my own power. I want to live in such a way that I am desperate for him to come through."[21]

ICNU

The first time I ever spoke on millennials, I was asked to be on a panel with a whole bunch of prestigious leaders in suits. And, well, I didn't have a suit. This was before the word millennial was everywhere, so most millennials didn't even know they were millennials. The word was still catching on. I'd often hear people call us millenniums. Which, heck, why not? Sounds like a cool spaceship.

Being new to speaking, I felt a huge pressure, because the conference, Movement Day, was a big deal with tons of leaders from Dallas. Of all the speakers, I was the only twentysomething, so I put in due diligence to know what I was talking about. I knew I had an uphill battle because my generation already comes with a lot of baggage and negative connotations. So I decided to find a key verse, which led me to the most popular young adult verse in the Bible. You've read it before. But here it is for your reading pleasure. "Don't let anyone look down on you because you are young, but set an example for the believers in speech, in conduct, in love, in faith and in purity" (1 Tim. 4:12).

I was going to go in and let the crowd know that young people needed more love and less lip. This was such a brilliant plan . . . until God got involved.

I think it's so ironic that young people mostly point to this verse in self-defense. But that's what I fell victim to, until I saw the most inconvenient comma in the last millennium. There was a comma instead of a period after the phrase "Don't let anyone look down on you because you are young, . . ."

I used to think this verse was a charge to older people to respect younger people. But I realized it was actually a charge to young people to live respectable lives, especially among older people. Now anytime I come across this verse, I hear it saying something more like this: "Grant, you better not give anyone older than you a reason to disqualify you because of your age. Be set apart from the rest of your generation because Christ has changed your life."

If our speech, conduct, love, faith, or purity is questionable, then we've given older generations reason to look down on us. We've given them a free pass to dismiss what we say because our words don't line up with our actions. Unfortunately, this is a fairly accurate snapshot of what young people have done. Millennials are not exactly known for our holy conduct, love, faith, or purity. And yet here we are, self-righteously shoving this verse into the faces of older people, when it's an indictment of us! It's kind of like a criminal shoving a warrant in the face of a cop.

If anything, we should not want older people to take notice of this text, because it serves to hold us accountable. Among young people, this verse should be treated like the Voldemort verse. The verse that shall not be named.

I never really read the whole verse carefully, let alone the whole chapter. Which, by the way, is a dangerous thing to do. We're pretty good at taking one verse and memorizing it, but we rarely know the full context. We all do it, though. Could you quote John 3:16 out loud right now? Try it.

Okay. Now can you do the same for John 3:15?

My point exactly. Good Bible reading, which I didn't do for a long time, always requires that we take seriously the context of every passage. So let's read more of this young adult text. "Don't let anyone look down on you because you are young, but set an example for the believers in speech, in conduct, in love, in faith and in purity. Until I come, devote yourself to the public reading of Scripture, to preaching and to teaching. Do not neglect your gift, which was given you through prophecy when the body of elders laid their hands on you" (1 Tim. 4:12–14).

Did you notice something? Just two verses after the most well-known young adult verse, "Don't let anyone look down on you because you are young" (v. 12), is a verse that includes older generations: "Do not neglect your gift, which was given you through prophecy when the body of elders laid their hands on you" (v. 14). How ironic. It doesn't take but two verses from the young adult verse until the Bible brings up older and wiser people. This verse doesn't just mention elders; it shows that they are essential to young people knowing and understanding their unique gifting. Without elders, Timothy wouldn't know his gift; therefore he'd neglect it.

This is happening all over the church right now. Young people are wasting their single years still searching for their gift, instead of fanning it into flame.

What this means is that 1 Timothy 4:12, the most popular young adult verse, is not actually a young adult verse at all. It is a multigenerational verse.

> Young people are wasting their single years still searching for their gift, instead of fanning it into flame.

A HAND ON MY SHOULDER

Months after my salvation, I was asked to share at a community Bible study. I had grown a lot that year since coming to know Christ, but I still felt very new to the faith. I remember reading Matthew for the first time and just soaking in the stories about Jesus. But then I read Mark and thought, *Yo . . . what's the deal? This is the same story. What's up with that?* I also remember that year reading about Saul and David and thinking that was Paul's story prior to being saved by Jesus on the road to Damascus. I knew Saul became Paul, but I didn't know there were two Sauls.

Needless to say, I was extremely nervous to share that night, because my biblical literacy was limited. I wish I could tell you that God descended upon me like a tongue of fire at Pentecost and I delivered the most incredible sermon ever. But I didn't.

Someone recorded it and put it on YouTube. So whenever I need a nice slice of humble pie, I go back and watch the video. Few things make me laugh hysterically or cringe unbearably more than watching this video. It was definitely a childlike faith, which isn't bad. But I needed a lot more of God's knowledge and wisdom if I was going to lead anyone.

CHAPTER 16, "MY FIRST TIME SPEAKING"

But here's the surprising part. After I spoke, an older man came up to me, pulled me aside, and put his hand on my shoulder in a grandfatherly way. He looked me in the eye and said, "Son, I really think you should consider seminary. You have a gift for communicating to your generation."

I haven't seen that man again. I don't even know his name. But I have never forgotten that moment. And I never will.

I doubt he has any idea what kind of power he spoke over me that day. I didn't even know what seminary was! One day I want to sit down with that man in heaven and point to the fruit of his ministry. I want to tell him my story and how my life played out. I want to introduce him to people whose lives were changed because of my speaking into my generation. I want to tell him that I got into college a week before it started, in a "coincidental" series of events. That small college happened to be a brand-new expansion to a local seminary. That man didn't just impact my life; he impacted many lives simply by speaking life into my gifting.

Paul brings up discipleship while speaking life into Timothy's gift: "I am reminded of your sincere faith, which first lived in your grandmother Lois and in your mother Eunice and, I am persuaded, now lives in you also. For this reason I remind you to fan into flame the gift of God, which is in you through the laying on of my hands" (2 Tim. 1:5–6).

This is the second time we see this idea that a gift is called out of someone through prophecy and prayer. I can't tell you how many people have prayed over me since I was sixteen and received my first gift-giving prayer. I'm not saying you can't be gifted without it, but I am saying it doesn't hurt to be gifted with it.

When that man laid his hand on my shoulder, he fanned into flame the gift of God. That man prophesied over me, and his prophecy helped to make me who I am today.

ICNU

The word prophecy can be scary. But sometimes it's as simple as four letters: ICNU.

I use it as shorthand for a powerful sentence older people can say to younger people: "I see in you . . ."

It's a powerful thing when someone older than you notices something unique in you. I had heard other young people compliment my gifting, but it was radically different to have someone who's been around and seen a few things tell me that I had a gift. Having that older man tell me what he saw in me was a milestone moment in my calling.

> The word prophecy can be scary. But sometimes it's as simple as four letters: ICNU.

When was the last time you told someone young, "ICNU"?

Words have power. I bet you can remember times when you were a kid and someone noticed something in you. You just don't forget that stuff. I bet there are young people in your home, office, or church who are dying to do something significant. What if Christians were the ones to speak into these callings? What if we could better channel these passions, not just for good but for God?

Here's the scary thing. If the church doesn't speak purpose into young people's talent, then I promise you, the world will.

Obsessive Comparison Disorder

My favorite movie is *It's a Wonderful Life*. I think the main character, George Bailey, is a great example of most millennials. But he also symbolizes what can happen when young people, with limited wisdom, make their own plans.

George, like many millennials, is so passionate. So confident. So purpose oriented. And so very social. He doesn't know exactly what he's going to do, but he knows it's going to be awesome!

In the film, there's an old abandoned house that George and Mary use to make a wish. You have to throw a rock, and if you hit some glass, your wish will come true.

George throws the rock, and he hits the glass. Check out what happens next.

Mary asks him, "What'd you wish, George?"

George, full of energy, responds, "Well, not just one wish. A whole hatful, Mary. I know what I'm going to do tomorrow and the next day and the next year and the year after that. I'm shaking the dust of this crummy little town off my feet, and I'm going to see the world! Italy, Greece, the Parthenon, the Coliseum. Then I'm coming back here and going to college and see what they know. And then I'm going to build things. I'm gonna build airfields. I'm gonna build skyscrapers a hundred stories high. I'm gonna build bridges a mile long . . ."

Spoiler alert: George Bailey never gets to do any of those things. And I don't feel bad for telling you. You've had at least seventy years to watch this movie!

George, with all his pent-up passion, doesn't fulfill any of his dreams. What George does get to do is watch his friends go and do great things. Which crushes him. He never leaves his "crummy little town," and he feels stuck as he watches Mary go to college, Sam start a business, and his brother Harry become a war hero.

I have heard it said that comparison is the thief of all joy. Millennials know this well.

Millennials deal with comparison in ways their parents and

grandparents could never fathom. Keeping up with the Joneses isn't new, though. Comparison's genesis was in Genesis. It started in the garden when the Enemy tempted us to compare ourselves with God. Then comparison got the best of Cain as he observed his brother Abel. But comparison has evolved over the years, and we need to pay attention.

Here's what keeping up with the Joneses looked like thirty to fifty years ago. You notice the Joneses with their new car, their better yard, and their kid's new bike. Basically, you see the exterior of their home. But perhaps you're invited in to see that they have better furniture than you, they prepare better meals than you, and their kids are better disciplined than yours.

All this made you feel inferior, but at least the comparison was mostly limited to neighbors and friends. You didn't have to compare yourself with the whole world. Now, however, for this generation, comparison is unlimited.

I don't just see your home. I can see your breakfast, lunch, and dinner. Your office. Your friends at work. Your new child. Your vacation. Your thriving relationship. Your family time. Your concert experience. Your job. Your promotion. Your every single thing that makes you look awesome and me feel empty.

> For this generation, comparison is unlimited.

I am seeing all this in real time, moment by moment, as I sit at home alone scrolling through Facebook or surfing YouTube. What's worse is that all this is happening under the banner of the golden rule for social media etiquette: show your best; hide the rest.

All generations struggle with comparison. I just think this generation has more arenas to compare than ever before. This is something that must be discussed with young people or they'll live in constant comparison. Many times, comparing themselves with false realities. In Dallas, there's a term for young people who live beyond their means and show off all their excess. We call them thirty-thousand-dollar millionaires.

I think this generation has OCD more than any generation before. And I'm not talking about washing your hands a bunch of times. When I say OCD, I mean obsessive *comparison* disorder. Millennials are a generation being downright crippled by the nonstop lies of comparison. We start our day on Fakebook and we end our day on Fakebook. So no matter what we did in between, there's always going to be someone who did something better. This is why I followed Simon Sinek's advice to purchase an alarm clock. This keeps the phone out of my hands at the beginning and end of every day. Constant comparison is a horrible way to start the day. The days when I wake up or fall asleep without my phone are always better than the others.

Back to George Bailey and comparison. There's a scene in the movie where he's helped to establish a neighborhood for people who used to have to rent. It's a fun, meaningful scene, as they have a celebration for the Martini family, who can finally afford to buy their first home.

▶ CHAPTER 16, "GEORGE BAILEY MEETS COMPARISON"

Then enters his old friend Sam. Sam tells him all about what he's been up to in New York. To make a long story short, Sam has become uber-successful with his new business. George goes from feeling ecstatic, celebratory, and successful to kicking his tire with disappointment and frustration.

> People say millennials fear commitment.
> But I think they fear missing out.

People say millennials fear commitment. But I think they fear missing out.

George feels like he's missed his shot. Because of this, his passion and purpose begin to fade. It's replaced with grumbling, emptiness, and depression.

So many millennials can identify with that feeling. Life moves fast, and we haven't moved fast with it. Thus we find ourselves really discouraged.

These are a few lies I've found tempting to young people.

1. You have to make a big impact—now.
2. You have to leave to make a difference.
3. Everyone else is farther along than you are.

Here's the irony. George Bailey wants to be a part of something big, and he is. He just doesn't enjoy the ride. He doesn't see immediate impact, he doesn't get to leave Bedford Falls, and everyone else is farther along than he is. However, he does get to see what the world would look like if he had never been born.

He sees that his entire community is impacted by the lack of his presence.

His brother Harry dies.

Loving families don't have their homes.

Potter has a monopoly on the town.

Mary is a librarian.

His mother is alone.

All in all, the true nature of his community is fundamentally altered.

I'm a George Bailey enthusiast. Because I think he's a great example of what a true local missionary is. A local missionary is someone who is so committed to a place that without their presence, their community would look radically different.

The sad part is that he is a begrudging local missionary.

Like many millennials, George isn't grateful for his time in his hometown until later in his life. I often run into this with young people in Dallas. Our program takes some of the most talented young people in the city and challenges them to commit to the city. Leaving is alluring, so they need a vision to stay. It doesn't just help the city in the long run; it helps the young person who thinks they're missing out.

A local missionary is kind of like Jesus.

This is a man destined to save the world. In the Bible, prophecies speak about the day he'll come. Israel awaits their Messiah. He is the one who will repair all that is broken. He is the Savior of the world.

It's pretty ironic that the one person who has changed the world more than anyone stayed focused on such a small region of it. For being such a world changer, he really didn't visit much of it.

Maybe we need fewer world changers and more *local* world changers. Fewer young people waiting to leave and more young people willing to stay. Being transient is at odds with making an impact. Because you're never going to make a difference if you're always starting over.

> A local missionary is someone who is so committed to a place that without their presence, their community would look radically different.

Jesus changed his city, and in doing so, he changed the world.

Young adults can get antsy. They don't see immediate impact, so they leave. Christian young adults may be the worst, because they feel like they have some type of manifest destiny to change the world. I encourage you to challenge them in daily faithfulness and speak life into their gifting along the way. Maybe even challenge them to forget trying to figure out God's will for their lives. Life seems to work out better when we simply ask God, "Give us *this* day our daily bread." Notice that Jesus didn't say, "Give us this week . . ." or "Give us this year . . ." Just "Give us this day . . ."

In *Forgotten God*, Francis Chan said, "I think a lot of us need to forget about *God's will for my life*. God cares more about our response to his Spirit's leading today, in this moment, than about what we intend to do next year. In fact, the decisions we make next year will be profoundly affected by the degree to which we submit to the Spirit right now, in today's decisions."[22]

CALLING ALL COACHES!

Every year at Initiative Network, we have people apply to be "missional architects," which is our title for interns. They tend to be young college students who are hungry to grow and learn. I remember meeting with a girl named Ruhamma and another girl named Tiffani. We listed out how we didn't want this to be a typical internship, where they got our coffee and did our grunt work. We listed out the perks of our internship, which was designed to be a launching pad for them. Free mentors. Free conferences. Free travel to New York City. But do you know what excited them the most?

Monthly reviews.

They asked, "Wait, so you guys are going to give us feedback every month on how we're doing and what we could do better? *Every* month?"

"Yes, we are," I said. "We want to make sure we're always on the same page because it's a short internship."

"We love that!" They were excited and thankful to get feedback.

I left that meeting thinking, *Wow. Young people apparently haven't received feedback from trusted leaders.*

I've found that most young people were coddled by their parents, and now they're criticized by their bosses. So they've been coddled or criticized, but they haven't been coached.

This generation needs "calling coaches." They're hungry for them. If the church doesn't provide them, the world will.

Unlike critics, who just tell you what's wrong, coaches show you what to do differently. Unlike coddling, which won't let you fail, coaches *will* let you fail—forward.

> Millennials have been coddled or criticized, but they haven't been coached.

Critics throw insults from the stands. A coach is in the game.

A coach isn't just for you. He's with you. But he won't and can't do the work for you.

On the EntreLeadership podcast, Dan Cathy, CEO of Chick-fil-A, was asked, "How are you able to consistently get teenagers excited to serve?" (Note that 78 percent of Chick-fil-A's sixty thousand employees are young people.)

He said, "First off, we are dealing with an employment base

that is very different than we've had in prior generations in that we've got children who are being raised in single-parent homes. We know this inherently presents a lot of issues for society. We've lost the opportunity to build the emotional strength of character and values that were intended to be built inside of the family. So we have to kind of make up for that as an employer. We select operators that would provide the kind of role modeling we would like for our own children. That's really where it starts, with a strong, competent businessperson as the operator who becomes a kind of de facto parent, coach, and mentor. That's why we have such great talent coming in the door to begin with."[23]

What if the church was filled with fewer critics and more coaches?

What if older people in the church regularly said to younger people in the church, "I see in you . . ."

I bet that church would be full—and flourishing.

LEVERAGING OUR DIFFERENCES

When I was nineteen, I got invited to a men's Bible study at Cracker Barrel. My new friend at church, Larry, led the group. Larry was an older man who grew up with a totally different background than I did. We didn't have much in common, but I appreciated his raw and real faith. He wasn't a perfect man, but he didn't try to act like he was perfect either. He was a doer, and I liked that, so when he invited me to the men's Bible study, I immediately said yes.

They met at 6:00 a.m., and it was about a forty-minute drive for me. I'm not flawless in this area, but I'm pretty serious about my yes being yes and my no being no, so I showed up the next week at the Bible study. (I've found that so much of life is simply showing up when you say you will, with a good attitude.)

So I make the long drive, walk in the door at an ungodly hour, and see Larry seated at a table with ten other guys. In a booming voice, he says, "Grant, you made it! I didn't know your generation even knew what it looked like before sunrise." As you can imagine, this was like making an Android joke in front of Apple users. Everyone burst into laughter.

Larry was an alpha male. But fortunately, so was I. I decided in my heart that day, *I am* not *a typical young person! I'm going to join this study and make it every time before 6:00 a.m.!*

So I started showing up every week, and I really enjoyed it. At that point in life, I had experienced older mentors, but I had never been a part of a consistent community where I was the youngest in the room by at least twenty years. Larry and his friends were all chronologically superior to me. Like, way more superior than me. (Take that, Larry—I just called you old in an eloquent way.)

> When one man was vulnerable, it was like a door opened to a room where suddenly all the men were allowed to be vulnerable.

This Bible study messed me up in all the right ways. What made it so great was how real these guys were with each other about their struggles. It was contagious. When one man was vulnerable, it was like a door opened to a room where suddenly all the men were allowed to be vulnerable.

So we'd end each study with prayer, and you had to share what was making you anxious in the week ahead. I found myself sharing about my troubles with dating, writing college papers, and trying to find a job. These were very real problems for me at that point in life, problems that consumed my thoughts. But every time I would share, the men would respond in the same manner. Some guy would pat me on the back, in a caring but also demeaning way, laugh, and say something to the effect of, "Don't worry, brother. We've all been there. God's going to get you through it."

My problems never seemed to be that big of a deal to them.

So I started listening, thinking, *Okay, so let's see what their problems are. What do big problems look like when you're their age?*

Although there were many men in the group, ranging from forty to seventy years old, their prayer requests all had common themes: relationships, character, and legacy.

1. *Relationships.* Their intimacy with God, family, friends, and coworkers.
2. *Character.* Who they were becoming along the journey of success.

3. *Legacy.* How they lived their lives and what they'd be remembered for.

It was in that Bible study that I learned the difference between wisdom and knowledge.

Charles Spurgeon said, "Wisdom is the *right* use of knowledge. To know is not to be wise. Many men know a great deal, and are all the greater fools for it. There is no fool so great a fool as a knowing fool. But to know how to use knowledge is to have wisdom."

I realized then that while I knew a lot for my age, I didn't yet have wisdom, because temporary things were still able to capture my heart. It took those men laughing at my problems only a few times before I started to see things differently. They'd say to me, "If I could go back to your age, I would . . . "

That's when I started paying close attention to the end of that sentence. I became a student to their comments, and God gave me two verses to take to heart during that season.

- "Look carefully then how you walk, not as unwise but as wise, making the best use of the time, because the days are evil" (Eph. 5:15–16 ESV).
- "Teach us to number our days, that we may gain a heart of wisdom" (Ps. 90:12).

I didn't find it coincidental that wisdom and the use of our time are collaborators in both verses. I think young people and seasoned leaders have three commodities that really complement each other. Young people have passion and creativity, but our greatest commodity is time. We have time to do things that just become so much harder once you're tied down with a spouse, kids, and a mortgage. These are good things, but I've heard them referred to as golden handcuffs, because you lose certain freedoms.

Older people have networks and financial bandwidth, but their greatest commodity is wisdom. They've been around long enough to know what works and what doesn't.

Take a look at this chart for a moment, which summarizes the gifts of each generation.

Young People	Seasoned Leaders
1. Passion	1. Networks
2. Creativity	2. Financial bandwidth
3. Time	3. Wisdom

Do you see the potential of what could happen for both parties if we came together? God could leverage our gifts in such significant ways! The problem is that the Enemy has done such a great job of dividing us that we can't tap into each other's strengths.

1. *What if young people's passion could be connected to opportunities in seasoned leader's networks?* Do you know how many honorable, gifted, passionate young leaders I know who can't find a job to save their lives? Meanwhile, I'm constantly meeting seasoned leaders looking for these exact kinds of young adults to hire. I think, *Why don't they already know each other? They need each other, and their relationship would be mutually beneficial.*

2. *What if young people's creative ideas to reach the next generation could be funded and expanded by the partnership of seasoned leaders?* Angel investors are always looking for the next start-up that will take off among the next generation. They're looking for the next young Steve Jobs, Bill Gates, or Mark Zuckerberg. They're looking for the next Instagram, Snapchat, or Twitter. Young leaders don't necessarily have better ideas. They just have a fresh perspective. But here's what I've found. The world is far more intentional to invest in the next generation than Christians are. I pray this changes, because if the groups that are radically reaching young people for Christ can't find financial support (which I've found to be the case), then the most effective next-generation efforts will always be underfunded and therefore limited. Almost every revival, including the one led by Jesus and his disciples, was started by young people.

3. *What if young people didn't waste their time on things that*

won't matter in eternity, but instead sought the wisdom of elders? Young people come off pretty confident. We have an uncanny ability to wing it. However, we have one stumbling block, and it's no small matter. It's just a mere question, but it will stop us in our tracks. The most difficult and defeating question you can ask a young person is simply, "What do you want to be when you grow up?"

> The most difficult and defeating question you can ask a young person is simply, "What do you want to be when you grow up?"

Like Steve Harvey at an award show, they'll stumble all over their answer. One year they think it could be this, the next year they think it could be that. It makes them squirm. They just don't know!

I've seen seniors in high school stress over the question, but I've also seen seniors in college paralyzed by it. I'm sure we all know quite a few college graduates who are *still* trying to figure out their answer.

This is why young people need the presence and prophecy of older generations in their lives. On one hand you have a generation who wants to do something significant, trying to figure out life, and on the other you have a generation full of wisdom and life lessons. On one side you have young people who can't decide what they want to do with their lives, and on the other side you have older people thinking, *Oh, how differently I'd do things if I could only go back to your age.* You'd think these two groups were made for each other!

But the problem is these two groups don't spend much time together at all.

It's actually quite a brilliant strategy of the Enemy.

I used to think the Enemy's main tactic was to get my generation to fall into drinking, drugs, and lawlessness. But now I realize he's just tricked us into envy, shame, and aimlessness.

He may not be able to rob us of our salvation, but he can rob us of our potential. He doesn't need to get us stuck in sin when he can just get us stuck in life—wandering, waiting, and essentially out of commission. He can paralyze our passion by vanquishing our vision. He's trying to sideline a generation.

The Bible says, "Where there is no vision, the people perish" (Prov. 29:18 KJV). Notice, it's not without passion. It's without vision.

Passion led by vision. Time led by wisdom. That's what we need.

If without vision God's people perish, then we can only assume that *with* vision, God's people flourish. The potential of the church is limitless when we come together. The Enemy isn't afraid of big churches. He's afraid of unified ones. He isn't threatened when we isolate. He's threatened when we start becoming one.

> The Enemy isn't afraid of big churches. He's afraid of unified ones.

HOW DO WE BUILD A BRIDGE BETWEEN GENERATIONS?

So you may be wondering, "How do we bridge the gulf between generations?" I think we can learn a lot about building a multigenerational community by looking at what's worked when building multiethnic communities.

I've spoken on so many racial reconciliation panels the past few years. When something bad happens, we do a panel. We have a panel for every problem. They mostly look the same: a white guy, a black guy, an Asian guy, and a Mexican guy. Sometimes these panels are fruitful. Other times they aren't. It usually depends on whether we know each other beforehand. If we do, the conversation is always better, because we trust one another and push one another into the uncomfortable conversations that need to take place. It's much harder to do that with strangers. However, Facebook posts, panels, conferences, and sermons cannot do the hard work of racial reconciliation. They can help, but they are fundamentally incapable of the heavy lifting necessary for the long and beautiful work of genuine racial reconciliation.

Two of my friends in Dallas, Jeff Warren (a white pastor) and Bryan Carter (a black pastor), are working tirelessly toward racial reconciliation, and they put it this way: "The gospel moves at the speed of relationships."

I like doing these panels, but after a while, God spoke to my heart, telling me that talking about racial reconciliation just wasn't enough. We needed to do more. I had no idea what God wanted me to do, so I started praying about it. "God," I prayed, "what else should we be doing during these divided times?"

> The gospel moves at the speed of relationships.

The answer came fast.

Watch movies about reconciliation.

Look, as I've already admitted, I love movies. *Love them.* So at first I just thought I was being lazy and wanting to do more of what I already love to do. But the longer I thought about it, the more legit the idea became—the more I believed this message was truly from God.

Think about it. Hollywood is far from perfect when it comes to morality, but they've done a pretty good job telling true stories of racial reconciliation.

This list leaped to mind.

- *Remember the Titans*
- *The Blind Side*
- *42*
- *Race*
- *Glory Road*

It hit me that most true stories about racial reconciliation are sports movies! Why? I think it's because teams require three things to build foundational trust among strangers. Even *Hidden Figures*, or a film like *Shawshank Redemption*, which aren't sports movies, have these three elements.

1. Shared goals that outweigh their differences (often a common enemy)
2. Unique adversity forcing diverse team members to rely on each other
3. Close proximity over a long period of time

Think back to *Remember the Titans*. One of the best. You know you loved that movie. At the start of the film, the racial tension is about to explode into violence. The city is on edge. The players are at each other's throats. Even the parents are adding fuel to the flame. Then the team goes to training camp.

Boom.

The three elements appear.

1. Shared goal: win football games. (Stronger than their disdain for each other is their desire to win.)
2. Unique adversity: no other school has a mixed-race team, and Coach Boone has been threatened with being fired if he loses just one game.
3. Close proximity over a long period of time: the coach makes black players room with white players.

Everything changes. The same kids who hated one another when they left for camp come back singing together. Upon seeing this, one of the parents asks, "What did they do up there? Brainwash them?"

Nope.

The coach did something better. He moved the team through the four stages of forming unity within a group.

1. *Forming.* The team members begin to get acquainted, and ground rules are established. Formalities are preserved, and members treat each other as strangers.
2. *Storming.* Members start to communicate their feelings but still view themselves as individuals rather than a team. They resist control by the group leaders and show hostility.
3. *Norming.* Members feel part of a team and realize what they can achieve if they accept each other's viewpoints.
4. *Performing.* The team works in an open and trusting atmosphere where flexibility is the key and hierarchy is of little importance.

Once you get your generations to come together and sing, "We are the Titans, the mighty, mighty Titans," then you've truly done something.

CHAPTER 17, "REMEMBER THE TITANS: UNITY IN DIVERSITY"

But how do we get there in our context? How do we build this among generations in the church? I think it's only natural for churches to think they need multigenerational small groups. And that may be the case, but I don't land there immediately. I think it's crucial that each generation has someplace where they connect with their own generation, and often that's in a small group.

But how can we be wise with the most relationship-heavy experiences in the church body today? What are the experiences in church that have a common goal, close proximity for a long period of time, and unique adversity? I'll point out four: mission trips, sports leagues, camps and retreats, and leadership teams and committees.

MISSION TRIPS

If you've ever been on a mission trip, you've experienced it. You leave for the trip barely knowing your fellow missioners, but you return BFFs. How does this happen? Why does this happen? The purpose of a mission trip isn't to make friends; it's to transform a community with the power of the gospel. But friendship—which is the epitome of trust—is always the result. Why? Because all three elements are present.

1. Sharing the gospel is a shared goal.
2. The trip provides close proximity for a long period of time.
3. Going on mission inevitably creates adversity, where people must rely on one another.

You're leaving the culture you've always known to collectively experience a culture that is nothing like yours. There's something about going on a mission trip that reminds you that the very thing you think is such a big deal in your world isn't a big deal in other parts of the world. This is usually a liberating experience for people. When you get back, others ask, "How was it?" But you just can't fully explain it to those who weren't there. There's a bond of understanding only among the group who experienced it together.

You also live together. When I'm with diverse leaders, I love anything where we're staying the night. As Christians, it's easy to put on a facade at a lunch or a meeting or even a full-day conference. But it's really hard when we're staying up till 11:00 p.m. and waking up at 7:00 a.m. Such a schedule in close quarters humanizes people, which creates sympathy and forges bonds.

So if mission trips are so relationship heavy, why don't we spend more time diversifying these experiences, both racially and generationally?

SPORTS LEAGUES

I love it when a Christian's competitive side comes out. Man, I am totally not the "let's just play for fun and not keep points" kind of guy. Having fun and not keeping points just don't belong in the same sentence. In my mind, they're at odds with one another. There is just some type of bond that is formed when you put people on teams and have them face off against one another. We just added the element of competition to our seven-month 72 Program in Dallas. We say competition creates culture, and culture creates community. Whenever you create teams to compete, you foster a place to belong.

I've never watched a full football game, but I feel like I've met a lot of professional football players. Every Monday I hear people say, "Oh, we lost last night!"

I think, *We? Did you actually play in a football game last night? Because I thought you worked in real estate.*

But people don't just support their team. They *are* their team. I've never seen men so emotionally invested. Entire weeks are ruined because "we lost."

So if competition brings people together, why not leverage this a bit to bring generations together? Not only does it build community, it's just downright fun.

> Not only does competition build community, it's just downright fun.

CAMP AND RETREATS

Camp and retreats are so generationally segregated in the church. But how cool would it be if we had college kids, seniors in high school, married men, grandfathers, and elders in the church bunking up together?

Show me a church that's doing that, and I'll bring the popcorn just to watch the Spirit work. I love it when God brings unlikely people together. He has a knack for it. I think we were designed for it. Our relationships shouldn't make sense without the cross of Christ. What if seasoned leaders in the church were strongly involved in volunteering at retreats and camps for young people in the church? Heck, what if *we*, young people, did a better job at including and welcoming them in our groups?

Leadership is lonely. But I think it's even lonelier for young Christian leaders because our generation is so disconnected from the faith. In response to this disconnect, I recently gathered young Christian influencers from across the nation for a retreat in Estes

Park, Colorado. It was incredible! But one thing I made sure to do was be intentional about having some older leaders there, guys who could act like guides to us. This retreat included Eric Swanson (missional awesome dude) and Dimas Salaberrios (former drug dealer turned prayer warrior), Scott Sheppard (genius city-collaborator), and Sammy Lopez (national speaker and chief encourager). These guys made the experience so much better. They added character to everything we did. Although they may have been a little older than us, I knew they were very excited about the next generation and the future of the church. They laughed with us, cried with us, and ultimately just invested in us. Eric Swanson cooked incredible meals of salmon, steak, pasta, and brownies with ice cream for dessert. If it had been just us young guys, we would have been eating Chex mix and turkey sandwiches. (I've done a potluck dinner with our 72 Group, and I kid you not—people brought Chick-fil-A, Pizza Hut, Wingstop, Taco Bell, Subway, KFC, and someone even had Chinese food delivered! It was hilarious and sad all at the same time.)

> The bonds formed during these heightened experiences go home with us and work to bring us closer together.

These men elevated the experience for us. And I like to think we elevated the experience for them. What's great about all these vehicles for building relationships, whether they're mission trips, sports leagues, or retreats, is that the experience is just the beginning. It's never the end. The bonds formed during these heightened experiences go home with us and work to bring us closer together.

▶ Chapter 17, "Leaving As Strangers, Returning As Family"

LEADERSHIP TEAMS AND COMMITTEES

Something special happens when people solve problems and face adversity together. I know something special also happens when people study the Bible together, but I would like to highlight the value of working together.

I once got invited, with a few millennial leaders, to a meeting with the Texas Rangers' marketing and sales team. Their goal was to answer this question: "How do we get the next generation interested in baseball?"

They had a real problem in front of them, and I thought it was ironic I was there to help. Apparently, the average ticket buyer was a little over the age of fifty, which meant baseball was truly becoming America's "past time." If you haven't caught on yet, I

> Something special happens when people solve problems and face adversity together.

don't really watch much sports. But I *really* don't watch baseball. It's slow, it's long, it's about only two guys doing something most of the time, and it's the only sport where people will say, "Well, yeah, it is kind of slow, but I just love the environment."

Now, don't get me wrong. The environment is the best thing about baseball. The hot dogs, the burgers, the warm atmosphere from hanging out and talking with your friends. I dig it. But what the heck, the environment? We're talking about a sport here, not the vibe of a new coffee shop. Baseball is the only game I've ever seen where people check out for like twenty minutes to hang out and talk. When they come back, they're not even worried because they didn't miss anything.

Needless to say, I wasn't that invested in this baseball conversation. But as soon as the conversation started, it was clear they really wanted to hear our ideas. And they took suggestion after suggestion about what could make baseball more relevant to young people. We offered some great ideas, but we also gave some pretty ridiculous ones. Add a shot clock, cut some innings, create a marketing campaign behind "The Lebron of Baseball" so young people have someone to look up to. But what struck me during the process was that they truly appreciated our feedback. They enjoyed it. Instead of defending themselves or critiquing our solutions, they kept asking for more ideas and took note of what we said.

After an hour or so of their gladly taking our feedback and ideas, I found myself starting to care. For the first time ever, I was interested in baseball. I wanted our ideas to work. I wanted them to try them.

Oh no. They got me.

People help maintain whatever they help create.

They first received our critiques, and then they received our ideas. Ask anybody who's started a business or executed a new idea. They'll do whatever is necessary, no matter how small or large, to get the job done and see their business succeed or their idea come to fruition. Their neck is on the line. Every church planter knows what it's like to put out the chairs. Every entrepreneur knows what it's like to fund their own start-up. If you're going to start a new thing, you'll do whatever is necessary to make it happen.

> People help maintain whatever they help create.

I wonder what young people are helping to create in your church. Have they been invited to the table to make big decisions or at least influence them? It's an important question, because the last place you want to be is where your young people have no real influence in the church and therefore no real commitment to it.

Many churches don't consider young people for staff and leadership positions unless they are married, have gone to seminary, and have years of ministry experience. The problem with this narrow view is that it disqualifies young singles. It also disqualifies our friend Jesus. (Note: Whenever our rules keep Jesus out, we need to reevaluate the rules.) There are actually quite a few lessons to learn from King Saul in this area.

Many times, young people are entrusted with miniscule responsibilities, so if they fail, it won't cost the church much. However, Saul entrusted the entire fate of Israel into the hands of a shepherd boy who played the lyre for him. David had no military experience. No qualifications. Talk about putting your neck on the line for a

young person! Moreover, when we give young people responsibilities, we don't usually like it when they come in and want to change
things. But Saul allowed David to fight Goliath his own way. It
probably seemed insane to let a shepherd boy go fight a massive
warrior without armor, but God had been preparing young David
for this moment all his life.

Sometimes young people bring a new perspective that seems
absurd, until it works. Then it forms a new model. As we all know,
David triumphed over Goliath, and in turn, Israel triumphed over
the Philistines. Moral of the story: give young people responsibilities so big that it will cost you if they fail, but it'll change everything
if they succeed.

So again, are young people in your church given a chance to help critique problems and create solutions? If not, you're missing out. God has a knack for using young people. I wonder why his followers don't.

> Give young people
> responsibilities so big that
> it will cost you if they fail,
> but it'll change everything
> if they succeed.

I think this could even be
at the root of why young people are leaving the church. They don't
show up because it wouldn't really matter if they did or didn't. They
don't own anything. Nothing is on the line if they're absent.

If you want to generate momentum, build trust between generations, and create advocates for each other's decisions, then diversify
your leadership teams. Because there's no better way to leverage
each generation's differences than to solve problems together.

Conclusion

I want to finish with something Jesus said that no one ever talks
about. It's one of the most discouraging yet somehow encouraging
verses in the Bible. I've never seen a pastor preach on it. You'll
never see this verse on a coffee cup, a T-shirt, or a bookmark. What

is it? It's the time Jesus said, "Oh, how long will I have to put up with you people?" (Matt. 17:17, my paraphrase).

What's going on here? Well, the disciples have just come down off the Mount of Transfiguration, where they witnessed Jesus' power and divinity like never before. Yet when they were asked to heal a demoniac, they couldn't do it! And what does Jesus do when he hears of their failure? *Heavy sigh.* "You unbelieving and perverse generation," Jesus says, "how long shall I stay with you? How long shall I put up with you?" (Matt. 17:17). That is red letter! God, in the flesh, *led by the Spirit*, asked himself, "Oh, how long will I have to put up with you people?" Honestly, all parents have hit a point of frustration somewhere along the way and asked themselves this question. Maybe not out loud, but at least in their hearts. It's just the reality of parenting. It's also the reality of discipleship.

It's discouraging to know discipleship is so hard that even Jesus was frustrated with the process. But it's encouraging because when I get irritated with slow growth, now I remember: I'm in good company. Jesus was angry with slow growth too; he just didn't sin when he encountered it.

> When I get irritated with slow growth, now I remember: I'm in good company. Jesus did too.

I also remember that I won't see the full impact of discipleship on this side of heaven. Just like Jesus didn't get to see all the fruit of his labor while on earth. Let me prove it to you.

Imagine a scenario with me. You become a new believer, and you start reading the Bible for the very first time. For whatever reason, you start in Acts. In Acts 4, Peter and John are brought before the Sanhedrin and threatened and told no longer to speak in Jesus' name, but instead of hiding or praying for a hedge of protection, they and fellow believers pray for boldness to endure. Later, you see the disciples beaten and told never to preach again, but the disciples respond in prayer and the laying on of hands to establish new leaders over the growing church (Acts 5:40–6:7). In Acts 9:40, you see Peter get down on his knees to pray over Tabitha, and she is brought back to life! This leads many in Joppa to the Lord. You're challenged and encouraged by the disciples' faith. They're such prayer warriors!

Then your pastor tells you, "If you've never read the Bible before, you should probably start in the Gospels. There you can see the stories of Christ."

So you start reading the Gospels. You notice the same disciples from Acts in the Gospels. But you notice a distinct difference. You see the disciples are not able to cast out a demon; Jesus has to teach them that it can be done only through prayer. You see the disciples interrupting Jesus' time alone in prayer because they think the crowds are more important. You even see the disciples falling asleep while Jesus is sweating blood in prayer. Jesus rebukes them for the lack of prayer support. After reading these stories, you think, *Are these even the same disciples?*

Prayer is one of our biggest assets that Jesus never got to see the disciples take seriously, at least while he was with them. But once he left, this all changed. I truly believe that once he left, the disciples started asking themselves the age-old question, What would Jesus do?

What did Jesus do to strengthen his followers? Well, he prayed. So they prayed too.

What did Jesus do when he was busy? Well, he took time to pray. So the disciples learned to take time to pray too.

What did Jesus do when he was facing persecution and death? He prayed, so the disciples learned to pray too.

After Jesus left, the disciples put what they had learned into practice. They prayed, Pentecost happened, and the rest is history.

Just because you don't see discipleship growth today, or even in your lifetime, doesn't mean you haven't planted a seed that won't blossom later. The disciples went from punks to prayer warriors. The same can happen to the people you disciple.

I want to remind you, this book isn't so much about how to reach millennials as it is about how to be the church God always designed us to be. I just happen to believe that millennials are hungry for that kind of church. We're in an age when it's possible to impress Christians but not look like Jesus. But I believe he should be our scorecard and he should be our goal. Jesus is attractive to all generations, all races, and all socioeconomic backgrounds.

He is our Lord. He is our Savior. But he's also our role model. If you want to see revival in this generation, aim to live like, look like, and love like Jesus.

In closing, if at any point in this book you thought, "This kid has wisdom beyond his years," you're right. I do. I have wisdom beyond my years because I have mentors, not just peers.

I didn't write this book alone. Countless men and women helped me. You should totally go check them out. You can see just some of my coauthors in the acknowledgements page. I consider them coauthors because they helped me write this book every time they invested in me. They helped me write this book every time they believed in me. They helped me write this book every time their walk with God challenged me.

Sir Isaac Newton once said in reflection, "If I have seen farther, it is by standing upon the shoulders of giants."

I have had many, many giants in my life. And they've made all the difference. So my one challenge for you in parting is this: help someone see farther.

It just might change the world. It'll definitely change theirs.

Notes

1. Richard Fry, "Millennials Overtake Baby Boomers as America's Largest Generation," Pew Research Center, April 25, 2016, *www.pewresearch.org/fact-tank/2016/04/25/millennials-overtake-baby-boomers/*.
2. "America's Changing Religious Landscape," Pew Research Center, May 12, 2015, *http://pewforum.org/2015/05/12/americas-changing-religious-landscape*.
3. "Americans Divided on the Importance of Church," Barna Group, March 24, 2014, *www.barna.com/research/americans-divided-on-the-importance-of-church/#.V-hxhLVy6FD*.
4. "What Millennials Want When They Visit Church," Barna Group, March 4, 2015, *www.barna.com/research/what-millennials-want-when-they-visit-church/*.
5. David Kinnaman and Gabe Lyons, *UnChristian* (Grand Rapids: Baker, 2012), 11.
6. Rachel Held Evans, "Why Millennials Are Leaving the Church," CNN, July 27, 2013, *http://religion.blogs.cnn.com/2013/07/27/why-millennials-are-leaving-the-church/*.
7. Fred Dews, "Eleven Facts about the Millennial Generation," Brookings Institution, June 2, 2014, *www.brookings.edu/blog/brookings-now/2014/06/02/11-facts-about-the-millennial-generation/*.
8. "Better Quality of Work Life Is Worth a $7,600 Pay Cut for Millennials," *Business Wire*, April 7, 2016, *www.businesswire.com/news/home/20160407005736/en/Quality-Work-Life-Worth-7600-Pay-Cut*.
9. Elspeth Reeve, "Every Every Every Generation Has Been the Me Me Me Generation," *Atlantic*, May 9, 2013, *www.theatlantic.com/national/archive/2013/05/me-generation-time/315151/*.

10. Kinnaman and Lyons, *UnChristian*, 28.
11. Bob Ditmer, "Ever Heard of 'the Great Commission'? 51% of Churchgoers Say No," *ChurchLeaders*, March 29, 2018, *https:// churchleaders.com/news/322375-ever-heard-great-commission-51 -churchgoers-say-no.html*.
12. Jim Cymbala, *Fresh Wind, Fresh Fire* (Grand Rapids: Zondervan, 1997), 121.
13. BankRate.com, "Over 44 Million Americans Have a Side Hustle," *PR Newswire*, July 12, 2017, *https://www.prnewswire.com/news -releases/over-44-million-americans-have-a-side-hustle-300487024. html*.
14. "Competing Worldviews Influence Today's Christians," Barna Group, May 9, 2017, *www.barna.com/research/ competing-worldviews-influence-todays-christians/*.
15. The speaker was Mark Driscoll.
16. Kate Shellnutt, "33 Under 33," *Christianity Today*, July 1, 2014, *www.christianitytoday.com/ct/2014/july-august/33-under-33.html*.
17. C. S. Lewis, *Mere Christianity* (1952; San Francisco: HarperOne, 2009), 205.
18. Ed Stetzer, "Dropouts and Disciples: How Many Students Are Really Leaving the Church?" *Christianity Today*, May 14, 2014, *www.christianitytoday.com/edstetzer/2014/may/dropouts-and -disciples-how-many-students-are-really-leaving.html*.
19. "Is Evangelism Going out of Style?" Barna Group, December 17, 2013, *www.barna.com/research/is-evangelism-going-out-of-style/*.
20. "'You've Got to Find What You Love,' Jobs Says," Stanford University, June 14, 2005, *https://news.stanford.edu/2005/06/14/ jobs-061505/*.
21. Francis Chan, *Forgotten God* (Colorado Springs: Cook, 2009), 142.
22. Ibid., 119, emphasis in original.
23. "Servant Leadership with Dan Cathy," *EntreLeadership Podcast*, September 27, 2011, *http://entreleadershippodcast.entreleadership. libsynpro.com/servant-leadership-with-dan-cathy*.